# UNDER COCONUT SKIES

*To my maternal grandparents, Julita Lopez Umali
and Abelardo Tolentino Morillo, whom my mother
loved so much and I knew briefly but sweetly.
To where it all began.*

# UNDER COCONUT SKIES

## Feasts & Stories from the Philippines

YASMIN NEWMAN

FOREWORD BY ALVIN CAILAN

Smith
Street
Books

Stirring the
Senses

Daily
Traditions

134

Natural
Beauty

194

Memories

FOREWORD
BY ALVIN CAILAN

# There's no more enjoyable way to learn about a person's culture, than to eat their food.

Philippine cuisine, as we know it today, has been treasured and preserved by the Filipino people since the early 1900s; and yet, in 2021, Filipino food still hasn't reached the worldwide popularity of other national cuisines. Why is this? Why is a culture so rich with history and pride only now finding its time in the spotlight? It's no secret that Filipinos are very proud of their culture, but when it came to sharing recipes and delicious dishes, we tended to keep those things to ourselves.

Growing up in East Los Angeles, a predominately Mexican–American district, I always invited my friends and their families to my family's parties so they could understand my culture. Ever since I can remember – birthday after birthday, Christmas and Easter – the bounty of dishes we served at parties or *fiestas* were always the same usual suspects: *pancit* (a noodle dish similar to chow mein); *lumpiang Shanghai* (spring rolls); and *lechon* – arguably an analogue for our many Spanish-influenced dishes – were the stars of the show. But these more 'relatable' dishes weren't the dishes that we ate every day.

I love Filipino food and I looked forward to dinner every night when I was a child. My dad would make some amazingly tasty food, such as *nilaga* (soup) or *tortang giniling* (beef omelette) and we'd always have fish sauce, *bagoong* (shrimp paste) and chilli vinegar

6   UNDER COCONUT SKIES

at the ready to take our dinners to a whole other level. But we kept these gems and flavours to ourselves instead of serving them at parties. I'm not sure why we did this. Was it shame because our food was humble or was it because as hospitable people we felt compelled to make 'accessible' food for our guests? Even our breakfasts, which I truly believe is the best breakfast food in the world, was rarely, if ever, served to guests. From *lugaw* and *arroz caldo* (both types of rice porridge) to my favorite, *longsilog*, a beautiful medley of Filipino *longanissa* sausage, served with fried eggs and garlic-fried rice, we have so much to boast about! But instead, my parents would serve bacon, eggs and pancakes to my friends when I had sleep-overs! I always wondered why?

Turns out, my Filipino colleagues all have similar stories, and I think this is what gave us the fuel to cook to 'real' Filipino food for our friends and to bring our cuisine to the world at large. And so nowadays, veteran Filipino cooks, who worked for some of the best chefs in the world and learned traditional cooking techniques from some of the greatest to have ever touched a saucepan, are now taking the lead and becoming a force in developing modern gastronomy.

Fortunately, we have emerged from the shadows and now have a platform to showcase our cuisine's finest dishes, as well as making innovative food with Filipino flair and flavours using ingredients not commonly found in the Philippines. The first time I ate *sinigang* (sour soup) at Lasa in Los Angeles, I was blown away: the chef used rhubarb as the souring agent instead of the traditional tamarind base. My friends were also amazed, and at that moment I knew that Filipino food had arrived.

People are now eager to learn about our food and taste our history through our dishes. Everywhere I go, people ask me how to make my *Bicol express mazemen*, which is a play on our traditional super-rich, super-spicy pork dish that I turned into a meat sauce and served with ramen noodles. In fact, I get asked how to cook Filipino food so often, I wrote a book about my *Amboy* (American Boy)-influenced cuisine. What an amazing time to be alive! Our food is here to stay, and the world has confirmed something we knew (but didn't always show) all along: Filipino cuisine is freakin' amazing. We even have statistics to follow it up! In 2017, two Filipino restaurants were listed in the top 50 in the United States by *Bon Appétit* magazine. In 2019, we had young Filipino chef, Tom Cunanan, win a James Beard award! And a fantastic Filipina chef, Margarita Florés, won Asia's Best Female Chef in 2016.

With all this new attention, we're now teaching people our recipes and traditions through cookbooks. It takes a special chef to take the time out and document our recipes. This isn't something new, but now our chefs and our cookbooks are more popular than ever! So, it's our time to shine and I'm proud to have helped carry the torch of Filipino culinary wisdom.

As with Yasmin's first book, *7000 Islands*, I'm positive that *Under Coconut Skies* will keep that fire burning, as it explores the ins and outs of Filipino cuisine, from the sweet, sour and salty combinations that make our food so enjoyable, to the herbs, teas and ubiquitous ginger and turmeric roots that provide great nourishment and bodily healing.

# 'Don't use that rice,' my neighbour warmly counsels. 'Use this one; it's sweeter.'

We take the bundle of *pirurutong* (black glutinous rice) wrapped in an old newsprint pouch from the market, soak it in water overnight to soften, then deliver it to Tito Felix, the sole guardian of a beautiful muted-red antique rice grinder in the village.

In the adjoining town, it's Tita Nenen. Hers is likewise charming, a 1950s engine with an aged chrome patina, and she's well known for her light-as-air *puto* (steamed rice cakes) made the traditional way with the wet rice flour from her old contraption. Light streams into her kitchen, casting striking blades through smoke from the woodfire below. Above, the tall wide-mouthed metal pot sputters and steams with rice cakes. It's the most perfect scene – resplendent and snatched from times' past ...

My grandparents' names were Julita Lopez Umali and Abelardo Tolentino Morillo. They had eight children, including the eldest, my mother, Ruby. As their descendant, a half Filipina-Australian, I am one of the 10 million Filipino diaspora joining the 100 million back home, whose hearts beat fiercely for our colourful land of 7,107 islands and never-ending smiles.

In the years since I wrote my first cookbook, *7000 Islands: Cherished Recipes and Stories from the Philippines*, immortalising the food and history of my mother's home, I have gone on to have my own children. As a mother, I yearn for them to know my *lolo* and *lola* (grandfather and grandmother) in loving spirit, and the pride and joy that comes from being a *kababayan* (countryman). While we live in Australia, we return each year to the Philippines to help sow this seed, much like my parents did for me.

It was during one of these trips that we found our own piece of paradise on Siargao, then a far-flung island in the country's south-east, where the rolling waves beckoned my husband and the small towns teeming with produce from the surrounding land and sea captivated me. Here, far from the capital Manila, I savoured the other side of the Philippines, where dishes were light, fresh and vegetable-laden, and artisan ways were preserved.

This is our native food, uncommonly fresh, simply cooked and requiring little adornment. The food of the Philippines that has sometimes gone untold in favour of the bigger, richer classics. It's often the case with simpler, peasant dishes and regional fare around the world, where you'll find untold ingredients, our ancestors' wisdom and the unadulterated taste of the surroundings.

Over three months, we lived in an aging but grand Filipino house by the beach and warmed to local life where everything you need is within hands' reach. Sweet young coconuts to drink each day or mature ones to grate and squeeze the creamiest coconut milk; banana leaves for tablecloths; *kaong* (nipa palms) for skewers; reams of *kalamansi*, turmeric, annatto and *malunggay* (moringa or drumstick tree) leaves to flavour and colour food; bubbling coconut vinegar to enliven and preserve it; rice from adjacent fields; green papaya and banana blossoms to use as 'noodles' and jackfruit for savoury dishes and equally for sweet.

In town, a few minutes' walk away, the *tabo* (local market) and *palengke* (public market) stocked fresh supplies: colourful fruit and vegetables grown in neighbouring farms, the daily catch brought in by fishermen and chicken and pork from pasture. In the mornings and afternoons, if you were listening, you'd hear the *tindera's* (vendor's) call — *mais!* (corn) *pan!* (bread) *pusit at sugpo!* (squid and prawns) — as they zoomed past on motorbike-cum-mobile stores with the day's specials from further afield, or the lilting trot of carabao as they headed to and from the fields.

I loved how if something wasn't there, you simply waited until it was, or came into season, substituting this or that and learning how to make do.

This is the essence of Filipino food, a cuisine characterised by a set of techniques not dishes. The *adobo* (braise) interchangeably made with chicken, pork, squid or papaya for meat, with soy sauce, fish sauce, coconut milk or nothing at all to counter the forward vinegar flavour. The *sinigang* (sour soup) of milkfish, prawns, beef shanks or pork ribs, soured with tamarind, cotton fruit, green mango or unripe tomato. Despite our own protestations that our mother's version is *really* how you make it, our *paksiw*, *kinilaw*, *tinola*, *silog*, *relleno* and *halo halo* are all designed for adaptability to what's on hand and endless variations.

This book follows in those footsteps.

It is a compilation of dishes and stories inspired by that vivid time on Siargao and travels to other distant regions, where bright, bold flavours abound and the vibrant bounty from the sea, earth and trees.

It is a tribute to the cooking found in new restaurants in the Philippines and homes of other second-generation and young Filipinos around the world just like me, as we proudly shape, share and champion our cuisine; a blend of classic dishes, regional fare, heirloom ingredients, plant-based reimaginations and different experiences we've tasted and seen.

It is a celebration of how Filipinos love to eat, with a kaleidoscope of flavours in each dish and an array of plates in each meal. The chapters, divided into feasts, reflect this vibrant approach and what we eat is inspired not simply by function, but also feeling.

It is the food from my kitchen that I invite you to eat with me — a mix of old and new recipes, to be shared at one big table, imbued with community, conviviality, family, myths and meaning.

Love,
Yasmin

*... Tita Nenen handed me a warm* puto *to try as she loaded the next batch into the steamer. It was soft and billowy as a cloud with the subtle fragrance of banana leaf used to line each mould. As I took a bite, the traditions that stretch back centuries flooded through me, as well as the countless new ones it has inspired.*

INGREDIENTS

Four main tastes abound in
our tropical landscape: sour, salty,
sweet and funk-bitter.

Found in the wild or readily extracted, they dominate and shape
Philippine cuisine in countless, multi-dimensional layers.
We also enjoy these tastes in vibrant abandon: forward,
complementary, juxtaposed and several sensations in each
mouthful. It's one reason we serve our meals with rice — a plain
tableau for a colourful painting.

There is a fifth and final taste we savour: *malinamnam*. Meaning deliciousness, it is the result of all the subtleties and combinations aligning. Here, nature and chef step back and the individual takes control, adding an arsenal of *sawsawan* — dipping sauces of sour *kalamansi*, salty soy sauce, sweet *atsara* (pickles) and more — to fine-tune a dish to their own taste and make it just so.

We say that wherever you go in the Philippines, you will always see the blue, yellow and green of our 7,000 thousand islands — the sea, the sand and the trees of our home. It's here you'll find the fruits, vegetables and herbs we use most, a blend of ancient ingredients found across South-East Asia and the Pacific, and new-world ingredients from the Americas. Rice, coconut, garlic, onion, tomato, chilli, lemongrass, turmeric, *kalamansi*, mango and tamarind, to name a few, along with the chicken, pig, carabao and seafood that we rear or that live in the wild. On windowsills or atop cupboards live our condiments and staples, also fermented or refined from the environment: *bagoong* (fermented shrimp paste), *patis* (fish sauce), *tuyo* (dried fish), *suka* (native vinegar) and *asukal* (sugar).

Among these are the less common, but vibrant botanicals and artisanal versions that add nuance and life. The leaves of *sili* (chilli), *kamote* (sweet potato), *kasia* (cassia), *ampalaya* (bitter melon), *gabi* (taro) and *malunggay* (moringa or drumstick), antioxidant-rich and medicinal. The sweet and sour fruit of *kaong* (nipa palm), *duhat* (java plum), *dalandan* (native lemon), *dayap* (native citrus), *santol* (cotton fruit), *kamias* (bilimbi) and *guyabano* (soursop), bursting with fragrance and extremes. The flowers, stems and weeds of *begonia* (purple flower), *alibangbang* (butterfly leaves), *alugbati* (purple spinach), *pako* (vegetable fern), *lato* (seaweed), *dampalit* (sea purslane) and *pansit pansitan* (edible peperomia), with intriguing colours, shapes and textures. The freshly ground *galapong* (rice flour), that's incomparable to its dried counterpart. The mounds of sweet *panutsa* (brown sugar cake) and dark and caramel *kinugay* (molasses sugar), that scream of the sun. Some of these age-old ingredients are forgotten among the pages of books or menus of big cities; others are at risk of being lost. Venture into the *palengke* (public market) of a small town or look in the surrounding gardens of people's homes and you'll see them used with imagination and vigour. Where meat is a luxurious commodity — for much of the country — they stand in as everyday meals: *adobo* with firm green papaya; *gina-taan* (coconut braise) with creamy jackfruit; and steamed banana blossom. Filipino food is often described as meat-laden and vegetable-bare. It's quite the opposite. The meaty *fiesta* foods once reserved for special occasions have become common-place in the capitals, but elsewhere our native, produce-driven fare reigns.

Rarer ingredients are also being revived in restaurants of young chefs paying tribute to the culinary heritage of our tropical backyard. While I've suggested substitutions for hard-to-find produce, it's surprising how much is now available abroad — not just frozen or preserved, but fresh, especially with a little enquiring at a specialty market or nursery, or the garden of a Filipino friend. It's a sign of the times that our ingredients are now being celebrated around the world. When you taste these unique flavours born of the land, the experience is a revelation.

INFLUENCES

'Philippine cuisine is a tribute to the
natural surroundings,' once wrote
Felice Prudente Sta. Maria, the revered
Filipino food historian and a dear friend.

In the ingredients, flavours and ways we cook, you see our beautiful island home and wild tropical landscape keenly reflected
back at you. We proudly call this our native cuisine — a salute to
our ancestors who learned from both necessity and resourcefulness how to master their environment in what was edible or not,
from the sea's weeds to the forest's leaves. They learned how to
preserve and also bring pleasure, and passed this down through
families and generations.

Our esprit for community and generosity, known as *bayanihan*, was also ingrained in the tribal communities of the past. It means that we take pleasure from preparing food for others, that our food tastes most flavoursome when enjoyed together and that we will always share what we have with you. Our food is a joint meeting between the cook and eater.

Philippine cuisine is also an edible account of history, with Malay, Chinese, Arabic, Spanish, Mexican and American influences, and millennia of trade, proselytisation and colonisation.

Simply read a menu for names that start a story: Chinese *pancit,* Spanish *kaldareta*, Mexican *tsokolate* and American mango float all share the page with indigenous *kinilaw*. There are hidden truths too; *adobo,* named by the Spanish for its similarities to their own *adobado*, is a native dish, while *arroz caldo* and *escabeche* are, in fact, Chinese in origin, renamed by the Spanish landed elite.

How we enjoy each dish also reveals past conflicts and accords. *Lumpia* (spring rolls) and *lugaw* (congee) share tables as everyday food, a sign that centuries of trade with Chinese seafarers and merchants was friendly and consensual. Our Muslim dishes centre in southern Mindanao, where Arabic missionaries and the word of Islam first arrived, making its way up the Malay Peninsula until the Spaniards pushed it back with Catholicism and the Spanish–Moro war. *Relleno, mechado, afritada* and *leche flan* live on as *fiesta* fare from 400 years of colonial rule. Mexican *tamales*, avocado, corn and tomato feel just like ours, brought from Acapulco to Manila on the centuries-long galleon trade when our native people were Spanish-governed. Meanwhile, creamy fruit salad is nostalgic, harking back to the second occupation of American forces and a time of mutual self-governance and assistance.

Taste each of these dishes and you'll also see our warm but proud heart. With each foreign arrival, we imbued our own traditions. To Spanish *afritada*, there's fish sauce for Filipino balance; to American pie, there's tender young coconut from the surrounding palms. Our native fare, by contrast, is fiercely protected. *Kinilaw*, our oldest known dish, is just as it always was with fresh seafood bathed in vinegar; *sinigang*, soup soured with tamarind from the land, remains pristine.

It grieves me to think some Filipinos feel ashamed, buying into a notion that their food is borrowed or what's theirs is only peasant fare. It goes some way to explain why Philippine cuisine generally has had a slower start on the global stage — a complex issue tied into post-colonial identity, which other countries likewise sadly endure. Now, first- and second-generation Filipino migrants are standing up, loudly, proudly and jointly in support of our cuisine, and it warms and inspires my heart to see. When it comes to our food, nowhere have I tried a collection of ingredients and flavours in such arresting forms as what you'll find in the Philippines — or anything quite as special.

With *almusal* (breakfast), *merienda* (morning snack), *tanghalian* (lunch), *merienda* (afternoon snack) and *hapunan* (dinner), we enjoy at least five meals every day.

Add to this *pica pica* (snacks), *pulutan* (beer food), *inihaw* (barbecue), *inumin* (drinks) and *panghimagas* (dessert), consumed almost as frequently. There is the food of our *turo turo* (local eateries), *karinderia* (restaurants), *lutong kalsada* (street food) and *lutong bahay* (home cooking), as well as our *ulam* (everyday food) and *pang pista* (*fiesta* fare). Yet this still does not convey the countless dishes laid out each time we sit down, and our wholehearted gusto for eating.

*Bayanihan* (see page 22) is behind the frequency and abundance of our food (along with a good appetite). With each meal to prepare is another opportunity to spend time together and show that we care. Food is our cultural language, crossing boundaries and imparting meaning not possible through words.

When we cook, we use a range of techniques to extract flavour. Our native dishes are predominantly elemental: preserved or swathed in vinegar (*atsara, kinilaw*), sour-stewed (*sinigang, paksiw*), steamed (*pinasingaw, halabos*), roasted (*inihaw*) and boiled (*nilaga*). The ingredients are typically untouched and naturally flavoursome. Our indigenous implements are likewise crude yet powerful and still widely used today: an all-purpose wing-tipped *bolo* (machete) for lopping and slicing; *kudkuran*, a stool with small metal blades for grating; clay *palayok* (pots) with hourglass curves that diffuse heat and infuse flavour; round stone *molo* for grinding; and bamboo poles, the environment's natural steamer with in-built chambers.

In a wide-mouthed *kawali*, a descendant of the Chinese wok, we use high flames to both stir-fry (*ginisa*) and deep-fry (*prito*) some of our favourite dishes, from *pancit* (noodles) to *crispy pata* (deep-fried pork hock). Today, our *kawali* is a pan for every occasion, to braise our *ulam* or cook our *almusal*.

We also layer and build flavour with *ginisa*, our version of Spanish *sofrito* with ample garlic, onion and tomato. This holy duo or trinity of ingredients, coaxed to life in oil, is the foundation of our stir-fries and braises and will make any simple vegetable or leftover taste good. Personally, I adore our gregarious use of garlic, made even more flavour forward with cloves in large chunks, simply smashed on their sides with the whack of a knife to flatten and release flavour.

In cities you'll find home ovens, but in provincial towns, there's still a proud custodian of a stone-brick equivalent to feed daily requests for soft, breadcrumb-dusted *pandesal* (bread rolls) and brioche-based *ensaymada*, as well as towering cakes, stuffed breads and sweet pies. Our beloved *panaderia* (bakeries) stretch back centuries to the sugar plantations and patisserie traditions of the landed Spanish and made ours with local twists and ingredients.

In each town, there's also a purveyor or two of our native *kakanin*. Made with glutinous rice, soaked overnight, then ground into flour or stirred slowly over low heat with coconut milk to render it sticky and glossy, these toothsome cakes are also an unboxing experience for the ages — wrapped beautifully in banana leaves in different decorative shapes. We gift these to the deities and feast on them for *fiesta*, as well as other tediously prepared and showstopping dishes: the deboned and stuffed chicken or fish *relleno*, rolled *morcon* and spit-roasted suckling pig, *lechon*.

I will never forget my time on Siargao, learning and practising many of these techniques, then cooking with the results each day — particularly old ways decreasingly found outside of small towns or reserved for the masters. Hand-pressing coconut milk, sun-drying cacao and naturally fermenting coconut vinegar rewards with pleasure and incomparable flavour. I still dream of the sweet, creamy coconut milk we made daily from *niyog* (mature coconut) fallen just outside our door and the unctuous Bicol express that we would make with it. This book is as much about the preservation of these wonderful traditions as new ways to enjoy Filipino food around the world, and I urge you to one day experience these wonders for yourself.

REGIONAL CUISINE

An archipelago of incredible breadth,
the Philippines boasts 7,107 islands, separated
yet bound together by water — inland seas
at the furthest points and straits and channels
at their nearest.

Together, its coastline is the longest discontinuous stretch in the world. The true count is said, poetically, to change with the tide, when islets disappear under water before re-emerging. Spread across this vast land and 80 ethno-linguistic groups is a shared heritage, as well as palate. Go anywhere and there's a version of *adobo, kare-kare* and *kakakin.* Yet in each small town and city, you'll find vibrant local cuisines, carved from their unique terrain and set of traditions.

The broad food strokes mirror our three geographical regions — Luzon in the north, home of the capital Manila and the country's rich *fiesta* foods; central Visayas, where sun-kissed islands teem with seafood and light fresh fare; and southern Mindanao, where Muslim not Christian traditions are observed and vivid spice-laden dishes can be found.

Explore further. In the harsh far north of Ilocos, bitterness is celebrated in dishes, such as *pinkabet*, where fresh produce is hard to glean. In mountainous Baguio, temperate fruit like strawberries blossom in the cool weather. Pampanga, home of the former Spanish colonial class, is the country's culinary capital with indulgent *pancit palabok*, *morcon* and *tibok tibok*. In Bicol, or coconut country, coconut cream and fiery chilli dominate from Bicol express to *laing*. In Batanes, dried fish and preserved pork speak to its isolation in sea and time. In Negros, where historic sugar plantations shouldered the country's early wealth, sweet *piaya*, *barquillos* and cakes abound and beloved chicken *inasal*. Cebu, the southern capital, claims the sweetest mangoes from the sun, and *lechon* laden with fragrant lemongrass. In Palawan, the untouched ocean produces the freshest seafood and *kinilaw*. In the southern food bowl of Davao, it's glorious durian, mangosteen, jackfruit and cacao. And in Marawi City, chilli is well worn and beloved in a spice paste known as *palapa*, a beacon of Muslim and Malay history.

Add to this celebrated local variations of Filipino classics: *pancit* from Malabon loaded with local seafood; Vigan *longganisa* with garlic and vinegar in place of sugar; *bulalo*, Luzon's heartier version of *nilaga;* and *tinola*, Cebu's less sour interpretation of *sinigang*.

Personally, my favourite notion of regionality are the charming specialties found across the Philippines and immortalised as *pasalubong* — food gifts from one's travels to share with loved ones back home. The carabao milk *pastillas* from Bulacan or the *buko pie* from Laguna; the pineapple from Cagayan de Oro or the *pastel* from Camiguin; the *kalamay* from Bohol or the honey from Bukidnon.

I've had the good fortune of visiting many of these places, from the small towns and far-flung islands to the historic, illustrious cities, and these few words far from adequately share the richness and wonder of our regional dishes and cuisines. In particular, little has been written on the Muslim food of the Tausug and Maranao people of Mindanao, and the tribes across the country, but local food writers and chefs are remedying this with new works and inspired dishes. A number of the recipes here are a showcase of the enchanting flavours and uncommon ingredients I encountered for the first time researching this book. I love that there is always more to learn and discover. Wherever you go in the Philippines, eat widely and curiously, for this is the adventure of food.

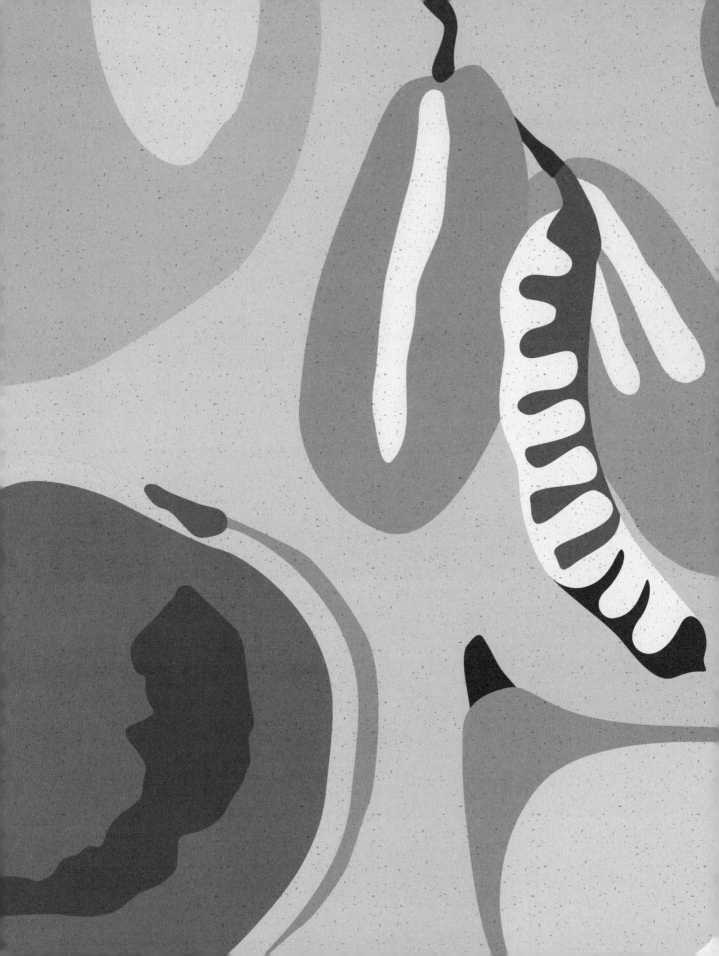

# CHAPTER ONE

# Stirring the Senses

FOOD THAT COOLS, WARMS,
SOOTHES AND EXCITES

### AGBIBITEN A PUSO (A HANGING HEART)
### MANGO

I love how the sun shifts from warming to ablaze in just moments as it wakes from its sleep below the horizon, or a downpour of rain sweeps in over a crystal clear sky with thunderous rapture. How the oversized leaves of banana trees shine in brilliant shades of emerald and lime, or the perfume and pungency of ripe durian weaves urgently through a crowded market. And how there is never a quiet moment, figuratively and literally, with lives lived side by side and intertwined.

In this equatorial land of a million beaming smiles, all senses are alive.

In the same way, our food elicits a bodily response. With each choice of ingredient and preparation comes a desired outcome. The tart *atsara* (pickles) that preserve and tantalise taste buds. The warming *sabaw* (soups) that whet appetites and cleanse palates. The sour fruits, leaves and native vinegars that help the body sweat and release heat, and the fiery chillies used for similar purging. The *salabat* (teas) that cure ailments and the healing herbs that extend life. The *sisig* that sizzles with fat for beer drinking or the alcohol steeped with fruit for *fiesta* potency. The *halo halo* that cools the body and brings a particular joy swirling disparate ingredients together. The *puto* (rice cake) as a *pampalipas-gutom* (light reliever of hunger). The pineapple dipped in salt for mouth-puckering *malinamnam* (deliciousness). And the dessert that ensures the last lingering note is sweet in more ways than one.

These are the dishes that cool, warm, soothe and excite — the dishes that bring us to life.

# RECITES

# Ginger & turmeric infusion with black pepper & kalamansi

## SALABAT

MAKES 1.25 LITRES
(42 FL OZ)

2 tablespoons finely grated
   fresh turmeric
2 tablespoons finely grated ginger
2 tablespoons raw or regular honey
1 teaspoon freshly cracked
   black pepper
2 tablespoons freshly squeezed
   *kalamansi* or lemon juice

In the cooler months, warm pots of ginger-laden tea, known as *salabat*, are made to ward off colds. It is one of a host of herbal concoctions and decoctions that are widely imbibed to boost immunity and heal, often prescribed by the village *albularyo* (herbalist) or passed down through folk knowledge. *Salabat* is also loved as a drink on its own merits, especially paired with sweet and sticky *kakanin* (rice cakes). I've savoured countless versions of this alluring and zingy infusion, here made with curative fresh turmeric, ginger, black pepper and *kalamansi*.

### METHOD

Place all the ingredients and 1.25 litres (5 cups) of water in a large saucepan and bring to a simmer over medium–high heat. Reduce the heat to medium–low and simmer for 15 minutes to infuse the flavours.

Enjoy piping hot or serve chilled over ice.

*Whenever I ask my neighbour for turmeric from her garden, expecting a knob or two, she arrives with a bilao (basket) spilling over with bulbous roots. Under the thin skin, the golden flesh beams with vitality, and a simple grating or pounding with the side of a knife yields ample juice and an aroma and flavour that's worlds away from ground turmeric.*

# Pickled green mango & jicama

## ATSARA

Next to every wonderfully fatty or fried dish, you'll find a tempting mound of colourful *atsara*. This tart, sweet pickle is eaten to cut through richness and offer a moment of counterpoint, encouraging the next bite of *lechon kawali* (fried pork belly) or *silog* (eggs and rice), or enjoyed simply as a snack. The most common variant is green papaya, flavoured with garlic, ginger, chilli and pineapple, but everything from banana blossoms to *dampalit* (samphire) can be transformed into mouthwatering *atsara* by steeping in native vinegar.

This is a less sweet version of my favourite *atsara* made with green mango (*burong mangga*), with crisp jicama added for its alluring texture.

### METHOD

Cut the green mango and jicama into 8 mm (⅓ in) thick batons. Alternatively, you can cut them into julienne (don't worry if they're not perfect, that's part of the charm). Place in a large bowl along with the salt and toss to combine (this helps to remove excess liquid). Transfer to a colander and set aside for 1 hour to drain.

Meanwhile, place the vinegar, sugar and 250 ml (1 cup) of water in a saucepan and bring to the boil, stirring to dissolve the sugar. Cook for a further 2 minutes, then remove from the heat.

Add the shallot to the green mango and jicama and toss to combine. Carefully transfer the mixture to a sterilised 1 litre (34 fl oz) jar, layering with the peppercorns and making sure you don't overpack the mixture as the brine needs to cover all sides of the ingredients.

Fill the jar with the hot brine, stirring with a knife to remove any air pockets, until the mixture is completely covered and sitting about 1 cm (½ in) from the top of the jar. Wipe the rim with paper towel, then seal with the lid. Set aside in a cool spot away from sunlight, for 1 week to pickle. Once open, store in the fridge for up to 1 month.

**MAKES 1 LITRE (34 FL OZ)**

1 large green mango, peeled
1 large jicama (yam bean), peeled
2 teaspoons sea salt
500 ml (2 cups) *sukang sasa* (nipa palm vinegar) or apple cider vinegar
110 g (½ cup) caster (superfine) sugar
1 Asian shallot, thinly sliced
10 black peppercorns

# Charred eggplant omelette with heirloom tomato salad

## TORTANG TALONG

There's something about smoke that can stir up our deepest memories; it's the primal act of charring over flames and the earthy, soulful flavour it leaves behind. It's the secret ingredient in our *tortang talong*, an eggplant (aubergine) omelette in name but elevated to so much more with its haunting smoky flavour. Quick and easy to prepare, we typically enjoy *tortang talong* for breakfast with mounds of warm steamed rice. I also like to eat it for lunch or dinner and this oversized version, topped or served with pickled heirloom tomatoes on the side, is a lovely dish to serve when entertaining. Much like a frittata, you can serve it warm straight from the pan or a few hours later when the smouldering eggplant flavour has permeated the omelette even more.

### METHOD

To make the heirloom tomato salad, place the vinegar, sugar and salt in a large bowl and stir to dissolve. Add the tomato and shallot and gently toss to combine. Set aside to pickle until needed.

Working with one eggplant at a time, place over a medium–high flame on the stovetop. Cook, turning often, for 5–6 minutes, until the skin is charred and the flesh is tender. Hold the stem and, using a fork, scrape off the skin, then gently squash the eggplant with the fork so the flesh spreads out but remains attached to the stem. Discard the skin. Repeat with the remaining eggplants.

Place the eggs and garlic in a bowl, then season and whisk until well combined. Heat the vegetable oil in a medium frying pan over medium–high heat. Add the egg and as soon as the base sets, add the eggplant, placing them flat side by side. Reduce the heat to medium, cover with a lid and cook for 3 minutes or until set.

Remove the pan from the heat. Strain the tomato mixture, reserving the pickling liquid, then spoon the salad over the omelette. Scatter with the coriander leaves and chives (if using) and drizzle over the pickling liquid. Serve with steamed rice, if you like.

SERVES 3–4

2–3 long thin eggplants (aubergines), stems attached
6 eggs
4 garlic cloves, crushed
sea salt and freshly cracked black pepper
60 ml (¼ cup) vegetable oil
large handful of coriander (cilantro) leaves
large handful of chives, cut into 3 cm (1¼ in) lengths (optional)
steamed rice, to serve (optional)

### HEIRLOOM TOMATO SALAD

2 tablespoons *suka* (native vinegar) or rice wine vinegar
¼ teaspoon caster (superfine) sugar
¼ teaspoon sea salt
250 g (9 oz) heirloom tomatoes, sliced into rounds
2 Asian shallots, very thinly sliced into rings

# Catch of the day with coconut vinegar, makrut lime & coriander oil

## KINILAW

'It may well be our national food,' wrote Doreen Gamboa Fernández, not of *adobo*, but *kinilaw*. The Filipino food historian was enamoured with the combination of seafood bathed briefly in native vinegar – liquid fire as she called it – which cures and preserves its sublime freshness. It's certainly our oldest: archaeological evidence dates it to at least 1000 years' old. Similar to ceviche, *kinilaw* is often made with fish, infused with the fragrance of *kalamansi* or *dayap* (native citrus) and made delicately sweet and creamy with coconut milk. But there are countless versions, a picture of local produce in each region and town. Inspired by Hapag restaurant in Manila, this fragrant *kinilaw* is set off with coriander oil and makrut lime.

### METHOD

To make the *kinilaw* liquid, place the ingredients in a non-reactive bowl and stand for 1 hour to infuse. Transfer to a food processor and blend until smooth. Strain through a fine sieve, discarding the solids. Set aside.

To make the coriander oil, place the coriander in a heatproof bowl, cover with boiling water and stand for 30 seconds or until dark green and wilted. Drain, then refresh under cold water. Squeeze to remove the excess water, then transfer to a food processor, add the oil and process until smooth and bright green.

Place the fish in half the *kinilaw* liquid in a bowl and toss to combine. Stand for 1 minute to cure, then drain the liquid and discard. Season with salt. Add the green mango and lime leaf and toss to combine with the fish, then divide among serving bowls. Pour over a little of the remaining *kinilaw* liquid, drizzle with the coriander oil and serve immediately.

## SERVES 6

500 g (1 lb 2 oz) sashimi-grade tuna or *tanique* (Spanish mackerel), cut into 2 cm (¾ in) cubes
sea salt
1 green mango, shaved into ribbons using a vegetable peeler
2 makrut lime leaves, finely shredded

### KINILAW LIQUID

125 ml (½ cup) *sukang tuba* (coconut vinegar)
2 teaspoons *kalamansi* or lime juice
60 ml (¼ cup) coconut milk
2 teaspoons sugar
½ teaspoon sea salt
½ small red onion, thinly sliced
1 cm (½ in) piece of ginger, peeled, thinly sliced

### CORIANDER OIL

1 bunch coriander (cilantro), leaves picked
60 ml (¼ cup) vegetable oil

# Open-faced sandwich with sweet & sticky longganisa

## LONGGANISA

*Longganisa* make my mouth water just thinking about them. Plump, stout, peppery and garlicky, our sausages are distinctive and addictive, becoming sticky and glossy as the thick-ground pork renders and the sugar caramelises in the pan. A descendant of Spanish chorizo, an imported ingredient during colonial rule, *longganisa* evolved using local ingredients and became a staple for breakfast alongside garlic-fried rice. There are few better ways to start a day in my opinion. I have another recipe for *longganisa* in *7000 Islands* made in the garlicky Vigan city style, but this sweeter, stickier version is what you'd describe as Kapampangan (from Pampanga region). You can use this recipe to make just the cheat's version of *longganisa* (no casings needed), but this sandwich is pretty delicious. Made with pickles and fried eggs, it's basically all the elements of our breakfast *longsilog*, plus creamy mayonnaise which we slather over all our sandwiches. I like serving it as an open-faced brunch board, but you can also turn them into individual burgers with brioche buns.

### METHOD

To make the pickled red onion, place the vinegar, sugar and salt in a bowl and stir to combine. Add the onion and toss well. Set aside to pickle until needed.

To make the *longganisa*, place the sugar, salt, pepper, fish sauce and 1 tablespoon of water in a large bowl and stir to combine (the sugar and salt don't need to dissolve). Add the pork, garlic and chilli (if using) and combine well with clean hands. Shape the *longganisa* mixture into six patties (the mixture will be quite wet, but will firm up in the pan).

→

### SERVES 4–6

60 ml (¼ cup) vegetable oil
6 eggs
400 g (14 oz) Turkish bread, halved through the middle, toasted
125 g (½ cup) whole-egg mayonnaise
3 bunches bok choy, stems and leaves finely shredded
sea salt and freshly cracked black pepper

### PICKLED RED ONION

60 ml (¼ cup) *sukang maasim* (cane vinegar) or rice wine vinegar
1 teaspoon white sugar
½ teaspoon sea salt
1 red onion, thinly sliced into rings

### LONGGANISA

110 g (½ cup) caster (superfine) sugar
1½ teaspoons sea salt
2 teaspoons freshly cracked black pepper
1 tablespoon fish sauce
600 g (1 lb 5 oz) minced (ground) pork
6 garlic cloves, crushed
1 bird's eye chilli, deseeded, finely chopped (optional)

Heat 1 tablespoon of the vegetable oil in a large frying pan over medium heat. Add three patties and cook for 1 minute or until the bases are lightly golden. Reduce the heat to medium—low, then cover with a lid and cook for 3—4 minutes, until the patties are completely caramelised on the bottom. Turn over and cook for a further 4 minutes or until cooked through and glazed. Remove from the pan and repeat with the remaining patties.

Meanwhile, heat 1 tablespoon of the remaining oil in another large frying pan over medium—high heat. Crack in three eggs and cook for 3 minutes or until the whites are set and crispy at the edges and the yolks are still a little runny. Remove from the pan and repeat with the remaining 1 tablespoon of oil and eggs.

Strain the pickled onion, reserving the pickling liquid. Place the toasted Turkish bread on a large platter or chopping board. Spread with the mayonnaise, then layer with the shredded bok choy, *longganisa* and fried eggs and season with salt and pepper. Scatter with the pickled onion and drizzle over a little of the pickling liquid. Divide into portions and serve.

# Fried chicken with banana chilli catsup glaze

## PRITONG MANOK

For us, fried chicken is the taste of happiness. It's memories of afternoon *merienda* (snacks) with friends and family dinners. It came into our consciousness in the early 20th century with the American occupation, when two fried chicken houses also emerged. Today, they characterise the two camps: crunchy Jollibee Chickenjoy or light Max's Restaurant-style. I chow into both, but when it comes to *pulutan* (beer food), a favourite food group in the Philippines, I can't go past the crust and shattering crackle of the former. As soon as it comes out of the oil, I plunge it in sweet and sticky banana *catsup* (ketchup) to glaze instead of serving it on the side, and douse it in *kalamansi* juice and fiery *sili* (chilli).

METHOD

Combine the onion, garlic, salt and pepper in a large bowl. Add the chicken and toss to coat well. Cover and set aside for 1 hour.

To make the chilli *catsup* glaze, place the ingredients and 1 tablespoon of water in a large bowl and stir well to combine.

Heat 1 cm (½ in) of vegetable oil in a large deep frying pan over medium heat. Place the flour and cornflour in a large bowl, season with salt and pepper and stir to combine. Working in three batches, remove the chicken from the bowl, leaving the onion mixture attached, and coat well in the flour mixture, making sure it gets into all the creases and crevices — the more the better as these will form the crispy crunchy bits. Cook the chicken for 2–3 minutes each side, until golden and crispy (or 3–4 minutes each side for drumsticks and 1–2 minutes each side for wings). Drain on paper towel, then repeat with the remaining chicken.

While the chicken is still hot, add to the glaze and toss to coat well. Transfer to a serving platter and squeeze over some of the *kalamansi* halves or lime wedges. Scatter over the chilli and serve with the remaining *kalamansi* or lime on the side for squeezing over.

SERVES 4–6

1 red onion, finely grated
6 garlic cloves, finely grated
2 teaspoons sea salt
1 teaspoon freshly cracked black pepper
1 kg (2 lb 3 oz) boneless chicken thighs, halved, or mixed drumsticks, wings and thighs
75 g (½ cup) plain (all-purpose) flour
85 g (⅔ cup) cornflour (cornstarch)
vegetable oil, for shallow-frying
5 *kalamansi*, halved, or 1 lime, cut into wedges, to serve
1 long red chilli, thinly sliced, to serve (seeds optional)

CHILLI CATSUP GLAZE

160 ml (⅔ cup) banana *catsup* (ketchup)
150 g (5½ oz) caster (superfine) sugar
80 ml (⅓ cup) fish sauce
2 long green chillies, thinly sliced

# Braised pork belly with coconut, pineapple & chilli

## BICOL EXPRESS

A few regions in the Philippines are known for their love of chilli, including Bicol, where Bicolanos add handfuls of fiery *sili* (chillies) to almost every meal. Synonymous with the region is Bicol express, a dish that some believe is named after a now-defunct train line that ran from Manila to the region; while others claim it's because you can run a similar speed to the train after eating this chilli-laden dish. Yet, this sweet and unctuous braise is not simply about heat. Starring *sili labuyo* (native bird's eye) and *sili tagalog* (finger chilli), the chillies are mild in parts, fruity and wonderfully colourful. It's also tempered by coconut milk, which renders into a rich oil, plus pineapple, traditionally cooked but served here fresh and sweet.

### METHOD

Heat 2 tablespoons of the oil in a flameproof casserole dish over medium heat. Add the garlic and ginger and sauté for 1 minute or until fragrant. Add the shallot, then season with salt and pepper and sauté for 4 minutes or until soft. Remove from the dish and set aside.

Heat the remaining 1 tablespoon of oil in the dish over high heat. Add half the pork, season and sauté for 4 minutes or until well browned. Remove from the dish, then repeat with the remaining pork.

Return the pork belly and shallot mixture to the dish, add the coconut milk, bird's eye chilli and half the long chilli and bring to a simmer. Reduce the heat to medium, cover and cook, stirring occasionally, for 40–45 minutes, until the pork is tender and the coconut mixture 'cracks' (the oil separates from the coconut milk); the mixture will become very thick, so make sure to scrape the base of the dish often in the last 10 minutes.

Add the coconut cream (reserving a little to serve) and fish sauce and stir for 1–2 minutes until warmed through. Remove the dish from the heat and season with black pepper. Transfer to a serving bowl, scatter over the remaining long chilli and serve with the pineapple and rice.

60 ml (¼ cup) vegetable oil
6 garlic cloves, crushed
6 cm (2½ in) piece of ginger, peeled, finely grated
3 Asian shallots, thinly sliced
sea salt and freshly cracked black pepper
800 g (1 lb 12 oz) skinless boneless pork belly, cut into 4 cm × 1 cm (1½ × ½ in) strips
800 ml (27 fl oz) coconut milk
2 bird's eye chillies, thinly sliced
6 long red and green chillies, deseeded, thinly sliced into rounds
200 ml (7 fl oz) coconut cream
1 tablespoon fish sauce
¼ fresh pineapple, skin and core removed, cut into 5 mm (¼ in) dice
steamed rice, to serve

*Each day at the local* tabo *(market), I am greeted by an array of* sili. *The selection is never the same — sometimes the chillies are tiny and fierce, while other times they are long and mild or bulbous and almost sweet. I love the shades of red and green, a rainbow of colour. The* tindera *(vendor) packages them up in old newsprint pouches for me to take home and smash into pastes or press in* sawsawan *(dipping sauces) for flavour.*

# Burnt coconut & lemongrass chicken

## PIYANGGAN MANUK

SERVES 4–6

4 chicken marylands
2 tablespoons vegetable oil
500 ml (2 cups) coconut milk
steamed rice, to serve

BURNT COCONUT PASTE

4 garlic cloves, finely chopped
5 cm (2 in) piece of ginger,
    peeled, finely grated
3 cm (1¼ in) piece of turmeric,
    peeled, finely grated
2 Asian shallots, grated
2 lemongrass stalks, white part
    only, pounded, finely chopped
4 bird's eye chillies, finely
    chopped
½ teaspoon sea salt
70 g (⅔ cup) Burnt coconut
    powder (see page 256)

The beguiling food of Mindanao is largely unknown beyond its borders in the country's far south. Fiery, heavily spiced and often dry and textural from curry pastes, the food is a reflection of our Muslim community and its historical ties to Malaysia. It also differs widely among the various tribes that make up the region. *Piyanggan manuk* is perhaps the most well-known dish of the Tausug people, made with their signature burnt coconut and chilli paste known as *pamapa itum*, which lends its alluring olive-black colour. It's an acquired flavour, but utterly unique.

### METHOD

To make the burnt coconut paste, place the garlic, ginger, turmeric, shallot, lemongrass, chilli and salt in a food processor and blitz to form a paste. Add the burnt coconut powder and blitz again.

Place the burnt coconut paste and chicken in a large bowl and rub well to coat. Cover and refrigerate for at least 1 hour to marinate.

Heat 1 tablespoon of the oil in a flameproof casserole dish over medium–high heat. Remove the chicken from the marinade, leaving a few flecks attached to the chicken and reserving the marinade. Cook the chicken in two batches, for 2 minutes each side or until browned. Transfer to a plate.

Heat the remaining 1 tablespoon of oil in the dish and reduce the heat to medium. Add the reserved marinade and cook, stirring, for 1–2 minutes, until fragrant. Return the chicken, along with the coconut milk, to the dish and bring to a simmer. Reduce the heat to medium–low and cook, covered and stirring occasionally, for 30 minutes or until the chicken is cooked through. Remove the chicken from the dish and set aside. Increase the heat to medium and cook the marinade for a further 15–20 minutes, until the mixture 'cracks' (the oil separates from the coconut milk); the mixture will become very thick, so make sure to scrape the base of the pan occasionally.

Serve the chicken with steamed rice.

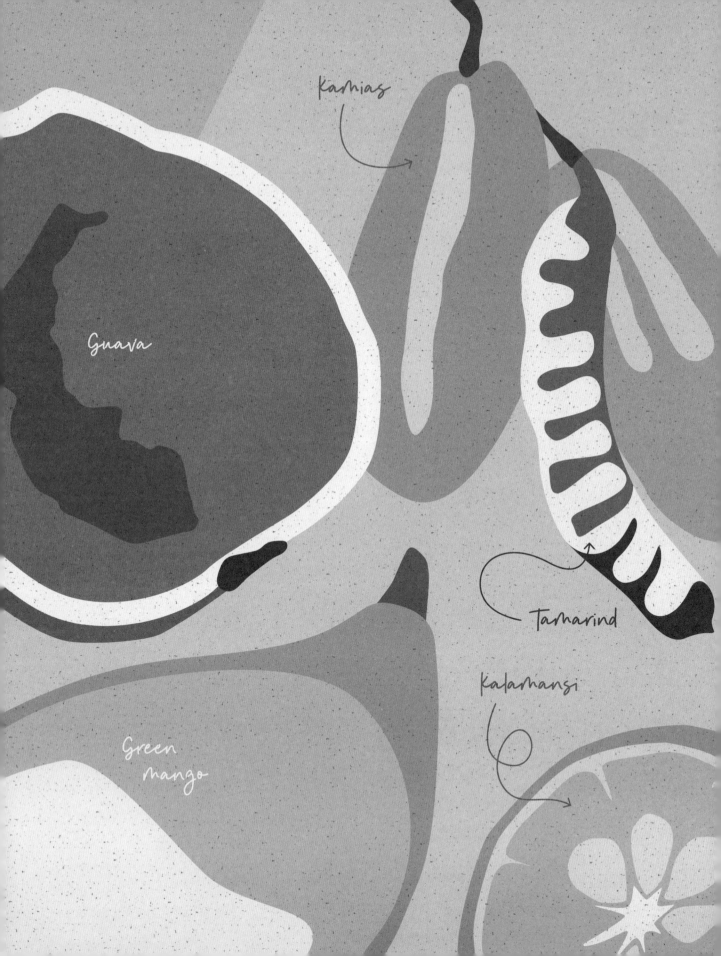

Kamias

Guava

Tamarind

Kalamansi

Green
mango

# Asim
## Sour

We say that sourness is in our blood.

Born of a landscape rich in natural sour flavours, our ancestors learned how to wield it: to expel bodily heat, preserve food and even 'cook' with it.

And, of course, for flavour.

We savour the almost imperceivable, delicate sourness of a mango bud and revel in the tingling, forward sourness of *suka* (native vinegar).

Our goal is just enough sour to make its presence known, but not too much that all else is lost — perfectly sour.

# Sizzling wild mushrooms

## INSPIRED BY SISIG

A regional Kapampangan dish of pork – typically braised, chopped, then grilled pig's head – *sisig* is traditionally served as *pulutan* (beer food). Its joy comes from the different textures on the plate, the anticipatory sizzling sound as it arrives on a hotplate and, truth be told, its dangerous richness. It's one reason it is increasingly reimagined with vegetables, and to great effect, and this dish follows in those footsteps. With a medley of exotic mushrooms in various shapes and sizes, it's stir-fried rapidly in a hot pan, with eggs usually swirled through at the end baked in like a shakshuka. It's light and fresh, with a *kalamansi* and native vinegar dressing, and beautiful to share as a vegetable side or main with rice, served straight from the warm pan.

### METHOD

Heat 2 tablespoons of the oil in a deep medium frying pan over medium heat. Cook the garlic and ginger, stirring, for 30 seconds or until fragrant. Add the red onion, the white part of the spring onion and finely chopped chilli, then season with salt and pepper and cook, stirring, for 4 minutes or until soft.

Add the remaining 2 tablespoons of oil and increase the heat to high. Add the button mushroom and stir-fry for 3 minutes or until starting to soften. Add the shiitake, oyster and king brown mushrooms and stir-fry for 2–3 minutes, until almost tender. Add the enoki mushrooms and stir-fry for 1 minute or until just tender. Season generously with pepper.

Reduce the heat to medium. Make three or four indents in the mushroom mixture and crack an egg into each hole. Cover with a lid and cook for 3 minutes or until the whites are set, but the yolks are still runny. Remove from the heat.

Meanwhile, combine the citrus juice, vinegar and soy sauce in a small bowl. Pour the mixture over the mushrooms to soak. Scatter over the spring onion greens and thinly sliced chilli and serve straight from the pan, with steamed rice on the side if you like.

### SERVES 3–4

80 ml (⅓ cup) vegetable oil
3 garlic cloves, crushed
2 cm (¾ in) piece of ginger, peeled, finely grated
½ red onion, finely chopped
2 spring onions (scallions), white part roughly chopped, green part thinly sliced
2 bird's eye chillies, deseeded, 1 finely chopped, 1 thinly sliced
sea salt and freshly cracked black pepper
300 g (10½ oz) button mushrooms, thickly sliced
200 g (7 oz) shiitake mushrooms, halved if large
300 g (10½ oz) mixed oyster, king brown and enoki mushrooms, left whole if small or thickly sliced
3–4 eggs
3 teaspoons *kalamansi* or lime juice
3 teaspoons *suka* (native vinegar) or rice wine vinegar
1½ tablespoons soy sauce
steamed rice, to serve (optional)

*'Let me unbox this for you,' says Tita Lani as she unravels the banana leaf pouch. Inside, glowing against the bright green is a bounty of wild mushrooms, plumped from steaming with turmeric leaves. 'The recipe is from the neighbouring tribe,' she says. 'They picked the kabute (mushrooms), too.' Sitting in a nipa hut on a vast coconut grove, this is Filipino food at its most beautiful, steeped in the fabric of the land.*

# Green papaya adobo with water spinach

## ADOBONG PAPAYA

*Adobo*, a technique for braising in native vinegar, is most often associated with chicken and pork, but our unofficial national dish also lends itself wonderfully to vegetables. *Adobong kangkong*, made with our ubiquitous water spinach, is a delicious common rendition, but at Bayatakan Farm, an exceptional plant-based farm-to-table initiative in the foothills not far from our home in Siargao, it is all about green papaya. Its firm, almost-meaty texture and beautiful glossy sheen elevates this dish from side to main, with turmeric leaves and mint adding an unusual and alluring undertone. *Salamat po* (thank you) to Analyn Dulpina, the wonder woman behind the cooperative and award-winner for her agricultural and community work, for introducing me to this simply wonderful dish and sharing its recipe.

### METHOD

Cut the papaya crossways into 3 mm (⅛ in) thick slices. Heat the oil in a large deep frying pan or saucepan over medium heat. Add the garlic and shallot, and cook, stirring, for 4 minutes or until soft. Add the soy sauce, vinegar, sugar and pepper and stir to combine. Add the papaya and turmeric leaves and bring to the boil over high heat. Reduce the heat to low and cook, covered, for 10 minutes.

Add the water spinach to the pan and cook, covered, for 1–2 minutes, until just wilted and the papaya is tender but retains some bite. Add the finely chopped mint, then stir the mixture to coat the papaya and water spinach in the sauce. Remove from the heat.

Transfer to a serving platter and scatter with the remaining mint leaves. Serve with steamed rice or fragrant leaf rice.

### SERVES 4

1 green papaya, peeled, halved lengthways, seeds removed
1 tablespoon vegetable oil
3 garlic cloves, smashed
1 large Asian shallot, sliced
90 ml (3 fl oz) soy sauce
3 teaspoons *suka* (native vinegar) or rice wine vinegar
1½ tablespoons white sugar
¼ teaspoon freshly cracked black pepper
3 turmeric leaves, tied into a knot (use Thai basil leaves if unavailable)
300 g (10½ oz) *kangkong* (water spinach), tough stems trimmed
1 tablespoon mint leaves, half finely chopped
steamed rice or Fragrant leaf rice (see page 180), to serve

*I always knew turmeric for its golden yellow root, but unbeknown to me, its long, green and fragrant leaves are equally potent — lemon-like and spicy. Analyn cuts off a handful swaying in the wind and ties them into a beautiful knot, then plunges the bundle into the bubbling braise.*

# Rainbow pomelo salad with peanuts & kalamansi

## ENSALADANG SUHA

When we eat fruit, it's not uncommon to sprinkle over or dip in salt flakes, especially if it's tart or bitter. This tempers the sourness, allowing the natural sweetness to shine, and enlivens the palate. This vibrant salad with two types of pomelo, salty peanuts and an invigorating dressing of fish sauce (or soy sauce if you're vegetarian), coconut vinegar, *kalamansi* and chilli is a tribute to this time-honoured tradition and our country's bounty of wild fruit. I'm always surprised that the blushing pink pomelo is the slightly bitterer of the two, and the yellow variety honeyed and golden, like sweet lemon. If you can't get your hands on pomelos, a mix of blood orange and grapefruit would look just as beautiful.

### METHOD

To make the *kalamansi* and chilli dressing, place the vinegar, citrus juice, fish sauce or soy sauce and sugar in a bowl and stir until the sugar is dissolved. Add the shallot, ginger and chilli and stir to combine. Set aside for 30 minutes for the flavours to infuse.

Using a large sharp knife, remove the tough outer skin and membrane of the pomelos to reveal the sparkling flesh. Remove the flesh segments, discarding the pith and membrane, then roughly tear the flesh into bite-sized chunks.

Place the pomelo and half the dressing in a large serving bowl and toss to combine. Drizzle over the remaining dressing and scatter over the peanuts. Serve immediately.

### SERVES 4–6

1 yellow pomelo
(about 1 kg/2 lb 3 oz)
1 pink pomelo
(about 500 g/1 lb 2 oz)
50 g (1¾ oz) salted roasted redskin or regular peanuts, roughly chopped

### KALAMANSI & CHILLI DRESSING

2 tablespoons *sukang tuba*
(coconut vinegar)
2 tablespoons *kalamansi* or lime juice
2 teaspoons fish sauce or soy sauce
2 teaspoons muscovado or dark brown sugar
3 Asian shallots, thinly sliced
5 cm (2 in) piece of ginger, peeled, julienned
2 bird's eye chillies, thinly sliced

# One-pan mung bean & tomato rice with crispy onions

## INSPIRED BY MUNGGO GUISADO

SERVES 6

When we think of comfort food, *munggo guisado* often springs to mind. This one-pan vegetarian centrepiece or side celebrates the flavours of our heart-warming *munggo guisado*, with pretty little mung-bean pearls strewn on top, crisp onion rings taking the place of *chicharon* and rice that's traditionally served on the side cooked in with the dish to soak up all the flavour.

### METHOD

Place the mung beans in a saucepan, cover with plenty of water and bring to the boil. Cook for 12 minutes or until the beans are tender, but still have bite. Drain and set aside.

Combine the flour and 1 teaspoon of salt on a large plate. Working in batches, toss the onion rings in the flour mixture, gently separating most of the rings. Heat 160 ml (5½ fl oz) of the oil in a large frying pan over high heat until very hot — it should sizzle vigorously when a test onion ring is added to the pan. Reduce the heat to medium–high, add the onion and cook for 2–3 minutes each side until crisp (adjust the heat if the rings are browning too quickly). Drain on paper towel and season with salt. Repeat with the remaining onion rings, adding extra oil to the pan if needed.

Heat the remaining 40 ml (1¼ fl oz) of oil in a 26 cm (10¼ in) diameter deep frying pan over medium heat. Add the finely chopped onion, season with salt and pepper and cook, stirring, for 4 minutes or until soft. Add the garlic and ginger and cook, stirring, for 1 minute, then add the tomato and cook for 2 minutes or until starting to break down. Add the rice and sugar and stir well to coat, then add the stock, fish sauce and mung beans and bring to the boil. Cover, then reduce the heat to low and cook for 15 minutes or until the water has evaporated. Remove from the heat and stand for 10 minutes or until the rice is tender. Season with salt and pepper.

Top with the crispy onions and herbs, and serve in the pan.

100 g (½ cup) mung beans
35 g (¼ cup) plain (all-purpose) flour
sea salt and freshly cracked black pepper
4 onions, 3 thinly sliced into rings on a mandoline, 1 finely chopped
200 ml (7 fl oz) vegetable oil, plus extra if needed
4 garlic cloves, finely chopped
4 cm (1½ in) piece of ginger, peeled, finely grated
2 large vine-ripened tomatoes, chopped
200 g (1 cup) jasmine rice
1 teaspoon white sugar
500 ml (2 cups) vegetable stock
1 tablespoon fish sauce or vegan fish sauce
coriander (cilantro) or moringa (drumstick) leaves, to serve

*The oil simmers gently in anticipation in its wide-sided* kawali. *The onion goes in, softening and sweetening, then the garlic, mellowing and enriching. Finally, the tomato, releasing its sweet red liquor. We call this* ginisa, *our sofrito, a flavour base brought to life in golden oil.*

# Watermelon ice with mango, coconut jelly & ube jam

## HALO HALO

Our most-loved dessert is arguably *halo halo*. A mountain of shaved ice drenched in creamy evaporated milk, this refreshing drink-cum-treat descends from Japanese *kakigori*. Consumed daily, it offers a hallowed moment of pleasure and reprieve from the oppressive heat. Made with a kaleidoscope of sweet and savoury mix-ins from *leche flan* to candied beans, *halo halo* (meaning mix mix, signalling the action of bringing it all together), is as endless as your imagination. This beautiful version with watermelon granita and coconut milk in place of shaved ice and evaporated and condensed milks is inspired by island life on Siargao, where colourful tropical fruit is always at hands' reach. For me, it's even more special served in natural bowls made from pineapple (as I have done here), baby watermelon or dragon fruit shells or young coconut husks, but it looks and tastes just as good in a traditional sundae glass or bowl.

## METHOD

To make the watermelon granita, place the watermelon in a blender and blend until smooth. Strain, discarding the solids and measure out 1.25 litres (42 fl oz) of juice. Place the sugar and half the watermelon juice in a saucepan over low heat and stir until the sugar is dissolved. Transfer the mixture and the remaining watermelon juice to a large container and freeze for 1 hour or until frozen. Using a fork, scrape the watermelon granita into ice crystals. Freeze until needed.

Meanwhile, if you'd like to make pineapple bowls, cut the pineapples in half lengthways, then cut out the flesh, keeping the skin intact. Reserve the flesh for another use.

To serve, divide the watermelon granita among the pineapple bowls, then top with the mango, star apple, dragonfruit or star fruit, lychees, *nata de coco* or *kaong*, yam jam, coconut, flowers and *pinipig*. Drizzle over the coconut milk and serve immediately.

MAKES 4

2 baby or small pineapples (optional)
1 mango, thinly sliced or scooped into balls
1 star apple, dragon fruit or star fruit, cut into wedges
handful of lychees, peeled and pitted
260 g (1 cup) *nata de coco* or *kaong* (preserved sugar palm fruit), drained
100 g (⅓ cup) Purple yam jam (see page 130) or use store-bought *ube* jam
1 young coconut, flesh scraped into thin ribbons
handful of butterfly pea flowers or other edible flowers
15 g (⅓ cup) *pinipig* (pounded rice flakes), toasted
625 ml (2½ cups) coconut milk

### WATERMELON GRANITA

¼ seedless watermelon (about 1kg/2 lb 3 oz), rind removed
220 g (1 cup) caster (superfine) sugar

# Creme caramel with roasted pumpkin & cinnamon

## LECHE FLAN

SERVES 4–6

*Leche flan* is our centrepiece *fiesta* dessert. When we hear its name our ears prick up and our eyes glimmer with excitement. Inherited from the Spanish and known elsewhere as creme caramel, our *leche flan* is infinitely richer — one reason it's so beloved. It's famously said that the extra egg yolks came from the overflow of egg white used as mortar to build our historic churches. The yolks give it colour and fat, and when cooked just so, gently in a bain marie, a smooth, silky finish. To top things off, our *leche flan* is further enriched with sweet condensed milk instead of cream. Conversely, when not delicately prepared, *leche flan* can be stiff and cloying. This recipe is my antidote. Inspired by an heirloom variation I discovered one day, *kalabasa leche flan*, its base of puréed cinnamon-roasted pumpkin adds earthy flavour to counter the sweetness, and body to prevent it from overcooking. Served in a pool of dark, almost-burnt caramel, it's truly irresistible.

### METHOD

Preheat the oven to 200°C (400°F). Line a baking tray with baking paper.

Place the oil, cinnamon, brown sugar and salt in a large bowl and stir to combine. Add the pumpkin and turn to coat. Transfer to the prepared tray, scraping any left-over good stuff over the pumpkin and roast for 25–30 minutes, until golden and tender. Set aside to cool.

→

2 tablespoons vegetable oil

1 teaspoon ground cinnamon

1 teaspoon brown sugar

pinch of sea salt

350 g (12½ oz) butternut pumpkin, peeled, deseeded, cut into 3–4 cm (1¼–1½ in) pieces

110 g (½ cup) caster (superfine) sugar

210 g (7½ oz) condensed milk

190 ml (6½ fl oz) evaporated milk

2 eggs

4 egg yolks

Meanwhile, place the caster sugar in a small saucepan over medium–high heat. Cook, swirling the pan, until melted and a dark amber colour (take care as you don't want it to taste bitter). Pour the caramel into a 20 cm (8 in) *llanera* (oval-shaped tin) or a 22 cm × 12 cm (8¾ in × 4¾ in) loaf tin and quickly swirl to coat the base. Set aside to cool.

Place the condensed milk and evaporated milk in a small saucepan over medium heat and bring almost to a simmer, stirring occasionally to ensure it doesn't scorch. Place the eggs and egg yolks in a large bowl and whisk to combine. Whisking constantly, gradually add a little of the warm milk mixture to temper the egg, then gradually add the remaining milk mixture until combined.

Place the cooled pumpkin in a food processor and process to a purée. Add the egg custard and blend until just combined (you want to incorporate as little air as possible to prevent the *leche flan* cracking). Strain the mixture through a fine sieve, then pour into the caramel-lined tin and tap on a work surface to remove any air bubbles.

Reduce the oven to 180°C (350°F). Cover the pan tightly with foil, then place in a large roasting tin and add enough water to come halfway up the sides of the smaller tin. Carefully transfer to the oven and bake for 50–60 minutes, until set with a slight wobble in the centre.

Cool completely, then refrigerate for 3 hours or overnight until completely chilled (the longer you leave it, the more hard caramel melts into a delicious puddle). Run a knife around the edge of the tin to release the *leche flan*, then invert onto a plate to serve.

# Triple chocolate tart with cacao nib praline

## INSPIRED BY TSOKOLATE

Our love for cacao stretches back centuries to colonial rule, when it arrived on the burly galleon ships sailing between Manila and Acapulco in Mexico. The rare fruit took readily to our equatorial landscape and we still favour it the way it was prepared in those days: tablets of roasted, stone-ground cacao beans known as *tableya*; and *tsokolate*, a thick, just-sweetened hot chocolate where the complex, fruity notes of cacao shine. With layers of chocolate crumb, dark and milk chocolate custard and cacao nib praline, this decadent tart is inspired by those ethereal flavours and the inventive *tsokolate* dessert at Lampara restaurant in Manila.

### METHOD

Preheat the oven to 160°C (320°F). Grease and line the base of a 36 cm × 12 cm (14½ in × 4¾ in) rectangular fluted tart tin.

Place the biscuits in a food processor and process to fine crumbs. Add the butter and blitz until well combined. Press into the lined tin to form a tart shell. Refrigerate for at least 10 minutes to firm up.

Place the cream in a small saucepan over medium heat and bring almost to a simmer. Place both chocolates in a heatproof bowl, then pour over the warm cream and stir until melted and combined. Cool for 5 minutes, then whisk in the egg. Pass through a fine sieve into a bowl, then pour the chocolate cream into the tart shell and place the tin on a baking tray. Bake for 25 minutes or until set on the sides with a slight wobble in the centre. Set aside to cool completely.

To make the praline, line a baking tray with baking paper and spread out the cacao nibs in an even layer. Place the sugar and 1 tablespoon of water in a saucepan over medium–high heat and stir until the sugar is dissolved. Bring to the boil, then cook, without stirring, for 5–8 minutes until you have a light caramel. Pour over the cacao nibs and leave to cool completely.

Finely chop the praline and scatter over the tart to serve.

---

SERVES 8–10

250 g (9 oz) plain chocolate biscuits
125 g (4½ oz) unsalted butter, melted, plus extra for greasing
300 ml (10 fl oz) thickened (double/heavy) cream
150 g (5½ oz) dark (55% cocoa solids) chocolate, finely chopped
150 g (5½ oz) milk chocolate, finely chopped
1 egg, lightly beaten

### CACAO NIB PRALINE

40 g (⅓ cup) cacao nibs
75 g (2¾ oz) caster (superfine) sugar

*As David lifts the hessian veil covering the wooden box at Auro Chocolate in Davao and stirs the fermenting cacao beans, I am spellbound by the sweet, funky perfume. Later, we drive to a plantation, where pink cacao pods hang delicately from the trees. A farmer tears one open and offers me the fleshy fruit, like sour custard apple, with the seeds soon to become the prized cacao bean.*

# Rum & mango two ways

Rum has a long tradition in the Philippines, a vestige of the vast sugar plantations established during Spanish colonial rule and a by-product of copious sugar cane. Tradition states that fruit be added to *alak* (a catch-all for different types of liquor) to increase its potency for *fiestas*, but the recipe for mango-infused rum – the first here of two – comes from my inspiring friend Mark Pintucan. As the director of Lokal, an NGO in Siargao, one of Mark's first initiatives was an inviting bar with proceeds funding other community-based projects. Here, a kaleidoscope of rums line the shelves, steeped and tempting with different fruit: banana, *kalamansi*, pineapple, cotton fruit. The sweet flesh adds not just flavour, but savour – cleverly masking the harshness of the Philippines' universal 30 *peso* rum. It's a wonderful hack to elevate any left-over bottle of rum you have on hand. The second recipe for baked mango drowned in rum is for your spiced or top-shelf stuff, with the natural sun-drenched notes of both fruit and liquor shining through.

### MANGO-INFUSED RUM METHOD

Place the mango in the rum by sliding it through the top (you may need to drink a little rum beforehand). Screw on the lid and set aside for at least 1 week and up to 1 month for a stronger infusion.

### BAKED MANGOES WITH RUM DRIZZLE METHOD

Preheat the oven to 180°C (350°F). Line a baking tray with baking paper.

Place the mangoes on the tray and bake for 25–30 minutes, until tender. Remove from the oven.

Run a small sharp knife along both sides of the mango stones to open slightly, then drizzle the flesh of each mango with 1 tablespoon of rum. Stand for 5 minutes to infuse and cool slightly, then slice into cheeks, drizzle over a little more rum, to taste, and serve warm with vanilla ice cream.

### MANGO-INFUSED RUM

- 750 ml (25½ fl oz) bottle Filipino rum, such as Tanduay
- 2 very ripe mangoes, flesh cut into 2 cm (¾ in) thick strips

### BAKED MANGOES WITH RUM DRIZZLE

- 4 mangoes
- 80 ml (⅓ cup) Filipino spiced rum, such as Don Papa, plus extra to taste
- vanilla ice cream, to serve

*A single glass is set beside a bottle of rum, yet there are many of us at the table. The first pour is given to the ground, my friend explains, as an offering to the spirits. He pours an equal measure to be imbibed by the next in line. 'Tagay!' we all shout and smile. It's refilled and passed along. This is how we drink until the night is over. We share the glass and our plate of pulutan (beer food) – a show that we are one.*

## *Sukang tuba*
## How to make coconut vinegar

3. Ferment in clay jars

2. Collect sap

1. Climb
coconut palm

4. Store and age

# CHAPTER TWO

Daily
Traditions

FOOD THAT BINDS

BULAKLAK MUNA ANG GAWIN, BAGO MO ITO KAININ
(FIRST MAKE A FLOWER, THEN EAT IT)
BANANA

I love the familiar noises that start and end each day — of coconuts grating and fish scaling, vinegar pots tapped and rice mats laid out, and arm-linked school girls giggling on their way to class. Equally, I love the silence that heralds lunch. A signal that slowing down is still sacred. Then, the beat starts once more — ladles knocking, barbecue fans flaming, tricycles whirring, vendors wailing and bellyful laughs as the sun sets and the heat subdues and dinner is savoured around the table.

It's no coincidence that the beating rhythm of food forms the sound-track to our lives. There are six official meals in our world and endless snacks in between. The rice *silog* for breakfast to fuel bodies through the day. The *banana-cue* (barbecued banana) for morning *merienda* and sweet pleasure. The saucy *ulam* (braises) for lunch at *turo turo* or *karinderia* (local eatery). The plates of *pancit* (noodles) for afternoon *merienda* to see us through to dinner. The garlicky *mani* (peanuts) at *sari-sari* (local stores) too hard to resist. The rich *bistek* (soy and citrus steak) with more rice for dinner. The deep-fried *lechon kawali* (pork belly) to complete beer drinking sessions. And *himagas* (dessert) for happy dreams.

With each dish, there's also meaning. *Lutong bahay* (home cooking) brings us comfort and family time; *lutong kalsada* (street food) is community. *Higara*, an ancient word, expresses food as pleasurable only with company, while *nayanaya* describes the implicit pleasure of feeding.

These are the dishes that punctuate our lives — this is the food that binds us.

# Sweet—salty redskin peanuts with fried curry leaves

## MANI

MAKES ABOUT 300 G
(2 CUPS)

300 g (2 cups) raw redskin peanuts
140 g (⅔ cup) caster (superfine)
 sugar
2 tablespoons vegetable oil
handful of fresh curry leaves
2 teaspoons sea salt flakes
2 teaspoons chilli flakes
 or 10 small dried chillies

Peanuts are our ultimate snack. They glisten in large vats at the market, just-fried with thick slices of garlic. They cover our fingers with salt from small bags sold by kerbside *tindera* (vendors) spruiking '*Mani, mani, mani!*'. They keep us upright when we drink beer, cooked with perky vinegar, pepper and chilli and paired with *dilis* (dried anchovies).

This recipe combines memories of our beloved peanut treats — the sweet, candied flavour of our peanut brittle, the moreishness of salt and chilli, plus fragrant curry leaves fried until crisp. For a sweet variation, you can swap the curry leaves for fresh *kalamansi* or makrut lime leaves. Or simply scatter with salt flakes. Either way, you'll be hard-pressed not to finish the whole batch in one sitting.

### METHOD

Line a baking tray with baking paper.

Place the peanuts and sugar in a large heavy-based frying pan over medium—high heat. Add 1 tablespoon of water and stir just to combine. Cook, stirring occasionally, for 2 minutes or until the sugar starts to coat the peanuts and the water evaporates; it will look like it's seized, but push on. Reduce the heat to medium and cook, stirring, for 10 minutes or until some of the sugar starts to caramelise; take the pan temporarily off the heat if it starts to smoke. Continue to cook, stirring, for another 10–12 minutes, until the nuts are candied — they will look rocky and glossy in parts. Spread over the prepared baking tray to cool.

Wipe out the frying pan, add the oil and set over medium—high heat. Add the curry leaves and sautè for 30 seconds or until fragrant and crispy. Remove with tongs and drain on paper towel.

Transfer the candied peanuts to a serving bowl, toss through the curry leaves, salt and chilli and serve.

# Fermented pineapple vinegar

## SUKA

MAKES 1 LITRE (34 FL OZ)

1 litre (34 fl oz) purified water
55 g (¼ cup) caster (superfine)
  sugar
skin, core and scraps of
  1 pineapple

Vinegar is at the heart of our sour-laced cuisine – and it's everywhere you look. It beams at us from big bottles infused with chillies at *sari sari* (local stores). It swirls in our small bowls of *sawsawan* (dipping sauce). Though now rarely practised, it relieves a dying loved one's pain, wiped on their lips as they pass from this world to the next. We call our native vinegars *suka*, an all-encompassing word for a swathe of different varieties, from the sap of nipa palm (*sukang sasa*) to the sweet water of coconut (*sukang niyog*) and the reduced nectar of sugar cane (*sukang iloko*). While these are the most common varieties, it's made with just about everything that contains natural sugar, including rice, cashew fruit and rambutan. Heat and humidity rapidly ferments the ingredients first into alcohol, then a vibrant living vinegar. The taste is wild, nuanced and unparalleled to commercial varieties, and absolutely transforms dishes. This is a natural vinegar made with the peels and discards of pineapple. It takes a few weeks, but it's easy and fascinating to watch it shift, funk and change.

### METHOD

Place the water and sugar in a wide-mouthed 2 litre (64 fl oz) sterilised glass jar and stir until the sugar is dissolved. Add the pineapple pieces and stir to combine. Cover with a clean cloth and secure in place with a rubber band. Set aside in a warm place for 1 week, stirring or gently shaking the mixture once a day to aerate (ensure the pineapple remains submerged in the liquid). Over the course of the week, it will bubble, get darker, smell funky and acidic, and a foamy layer will develop on the top.

Strain the liquid through fine muslin (cheesecloth), discarding the solids. Transfer the vinegar to a 1 litre (34 fl oz) sterilised bottle, cover with a clean cloth and rubber band and set aside for another 1 week to ferment. Once it tastes like vinegar, seal with a lid and store in the pantry or a dark place until ready to use. Once opened, it will keep in the fridge for at least 1 month.

# Charred flatbreads with moringa leaves

MAKES 6

300 g (2 cups) plain (all-purpose) flour, plus extra for dusting
1½ teaspoons sea salt
¼ teaspoon active dried yeast
230 ml (8 fl oz) lukewarm water
large handful of moringa (drumstick) leaves, pounded to a paste or 2 teaspoons moringa powder
1 tablespoon vegetable oil

Across the country, the town bakery is where you head for our beloved *pandesal* (bread rolls), soft and puffed from a brick oven. In some regions, you can also find crisp or stretchy flatbread, cooked quickly on street-corner griddles or hotplates over open fires. On Siargao Island, *malunggay* (moringa or drumstick) leaves are often added to the dough, tinting it vibrantly green, boosting it with antioxidants and adding an earthy, grassy undertone, with a sprig of leaves on top for charm. The best thing about this recipe is that you don't have to knead the dough; set it aside for a day and the long proof does the work. I've also designed it for cooking simply in a frying pan, the charred edges evoking those lucid charcoal fires.

## METHOD

Place the flour, salt and yeast in a large bowl and stir until well combined. Add the water and stir until incorporated (there should be no dry or floury bits, but the dough should have a bit of structure). Combine the moringa paste or powder and oil in a small jug, then knead into the dough until well combined and the dough is tinted green. Cover with plastic wrap or a tea towel and set aside at room temperature for 18–24 hours, until more than doubled in size. The time will depend on the temperature of your kitchen; warmer will be faster, cooler will be slower.

Flour a work surface and divide the dough into six portions. Working with one portion at a time, pull the right side of the dough up and then towards the centre, then the left, then the top, then the bottom. Shape into a rough ball, turn seam-side down, then shape into a neat circular mound. The mounds should not be sticky; if they are, dust with more flour. Using a rolling pin, roll each portion into a very thin oval shape; it's okay if the shape is irregular and a little thinner and thicker in parts — this gives it rustic character.

Heat a large frying pan or barbecue hotplate to high. Cook the flatbreads, one at a time, for 2 minutes each side or until puffed, slightly charred in parts and cooked through; they will be chewy and crispy. Serve immediately or cool to room temperature.

*Dotting streets are* malunggay *(moringa) trees big and small. I ask their owners for a few leaves, but they always break off branches and tell me to take as I please. It's our miracle plant, they tell me — wildly nutritious — and I should swirl it into soups or scatter over rice. Once snapped from its tree, the beautiful leaves wilt quickly, but there's miraculously a new branch in its place the next day.*

# Rice bowl with crispy garlic chips, chives & chicharron

## INSPIRED BY SILOG

Our breakfasts are deliciously heavy by design to fuel us for the day ahead, traditionally for long stretches on the field or out at sea. Our favourite iteration is *silog*, an abbreviation for *si + log* from *sinangag* (fried rice) and *itlog* (egg), brought to life quickly with left-over rice from the night before. It makes my mouth water thinking about the combination of hot oil, salt and garlic, and now young chefs are reimagining this classic, including at Toyo in Manila, where the inspiration for this recipe comes from. Here, the savoury soy sauce and runny egg yolks that are usually served on the side are cooked into the rice, with rich garlic oil rippling through it. It's simple yet wildly moreish and just as good for dinner.

### METHOD

Heat 2 tablespoons of the oil in a medium saucepan over medium heat. Add the finely chopped garlic and sauté for 1 minute or until fragrant. Add the rice and stir until well coated in the garlicky oil. Add the stock and soy sauce and stir well to combine. Bring to the boil over high heat, then cover, reduce the heat to low and cook for 12 minutes or until the rice has absorbed the liquid. Remove from the heat and stand for 5 minutes.

Meanwhile, place the thinly sliced garlic and remaining oil in a small saucepan and bring to a simmer over medium heat. Cook for 3–5 minutes, until the garlic just starts to turn golden (take care as it burns quickly). Remove from the heat and stand until needed.

Add half the chives or spring onion and half the garlic oil to the warm rice, season with pepper and stir through. Divide the rice among bowls, make an egg yolk–sized indent in the middle of each bowl and add the egg yolks. Pour over the remaining garlic oil, scatter over the chicharon or crispy fried shallots and the remaining chives or spring onion and serve immediately, stirring the yolks through the warm rice to coat. Alternatively, simply stir the egg yolks through the rice before dividing among bowls.

SERVES 4–6

125 ml (½ cup) vegetable oil
1 garlic bulb, half the cloves finely chopped, half the cloves thinly sliced
400 g (2 cups) jasmine rice
750 ml (3 cups) chicken or vegetable stock
80 ml (⅓ cup) soy sauce
1 bunch garlic chives or ½ bunch spring onions (scallions), thinly sliced
freshly cracked black pepper
4 egg yolks
15 g (½ cup) crushed chicharon (pork crackling) or crispy fried shallots

*As a child, I'd wake to the melodic sounds of garlic purring gently in oil and rice rocking against the high side of a pan as it became sinangag (garlic fried rice) — it too stirring from its slumber in the fridge. There was no need for mum or tita (aunty) to call out, the rich alluring smell was enough to say breakfast is ready.*

# Egg noodles with charred tofu & Asian greens

## PANCIT HABHAB

SERVES 4

500 g (1 lb 2 oz) fresh egg noodles
80 ml (⅓ cup) soy sauce
2 tablespoons banana *catsup*
  (ketchup) or tomato ketchup
1½ tablespoons white sugar
400 g (14 oz) firm tofu, cut into
  3 cm × 1 cm (1¼ in × ½ in)
  strips
60 ml (¼ cup) vegetable oil
1 bunch gai lan (Chinese broccoli)
  or broccolini, halved lengthways
  if thick, then cut into 4 cm (1½
  in) lengths
1 small red onion, thinly sliced
3 garlic cloves, thinly sliced
1 egg, lightly beaten
1 tablespoon *kalamansi* juice or
  lemon juice, plus extra wedges
  to serve
35 g (¼ cup) salted roasted
  peanuts, roughly chopped
freshly cracked black pepper

The delectable noodle stir-fry from Quezon province in the country's north takes its name, *habhab* — meaning to gobble up — from the way it's cooked and served — hot and fast in woks at the local market, then piled onto 'plates' of banana leaves for instant eating. I love these bustling, smoky scenes, with arms moving and flames roaring and whatever's on hand thrown into the mix — and it's the essence of this vegetarian version. As the tofu, greens and *catsup-kalamansi* hit the wok, they caramelise and char, adding layers of moreish sweet, salty and sour flavours.

### METHOD

Cook the noodles in a saucepan of boiling water for 3 minutes or until just tender. Strain, reserving 2 tablespoons of the cooking water, and rinse under running water to prevent them sticking.

Meanwhile, place the soy sauce, banana *catsup* and sugar in a bowl and stir until the sugar is dissolved. Add the tofu and gently turn to coat. Strain the tofu, reserving the marinade, then add the cooking water to the marinade and stir to combine.

Heat 1 tablespoon of the oil in a wok or deep frying pan over medium–high heat. Stir-fry the broccoli or broccolini for 2 minutes or until just tender and charred. Transfer to a plate, then add the tofu to the wok and cook, turning, for 2 minutes or until slightly charred. Transfer to a plate and wipe the wok clean. Heat the remaining oil in the wok over medium–high heat. Stir-fry the onion and garlic for 2–3 minutes, until softened. Add the marinade and bring to the boil. Add the noodles and cook, tossing, for 2 minutes or until the liquid has almost evaporated. Working quickly, add the egg and cook, tossing, for 1 minute or until the noodles are coated and glossy. Remove the wok from the heat, pour over the citrus juice and toss to combine.

Top with the tofu and broccoli or broccolini, scatter over the peanuts and season generously with black pepper. Serve with *kalamansi* or lemon wedges for squeezing over.

# Annatto roast chicken & shallots

## INSPIRED BY INASAL

If you live near a bushy lipstick tree, you have the good fortune of beauty and substance. Inside the striking crimson pods are small, but potent seeds known as annatto, or *atsuete* in our tongue. Once dried in the sun, then steeped in oil, the seeds release a vibrant hue and alluring aroma. Originally from the Amazon, the seeds arrived in the Philippines by way of the Spanish galleon trade, and while not widely used they are signature to some of our best-loved dishes, including a mouth-watering regional variation of barbecue chicken known as *inasal*. For this quick, weeknight version, I pop chicken pieces in a baking dish, near-drown them in annatto oil, then roast in the oven, intensifying the meat with caramelised shallots, garlic and chicken juices. For Filipinos, the resulting golden liquor is the equivalent of the lip-smacking chicken oil often served with *inasal*, as well as spiced vinegar, which cuts through the richness.

### METHOD

Preheat the oven to 220°C (430°F).

Place the chicken, shallot and garlic in a roasting tin lined with baking paper. Scatter over the salt and sugar, then season with pepper. Pour over the annatto oil and rub all over the chicken. Turn the chicken skin-side up and roast for 25–30 minutes, until the chicken is dark golden and cooked through (there will be lots of delicious annatto oil in the tray).

Meanwhile, to make the coconut vinegar *sawsawan*, combine all the ingredients in a small bowl.

Transfer the chicken and shallot to a serving platter. Gently press the garlic on the tray to release extra flavour, then scrape the garlic, pan bits and oil together to combine and drizzle over the chicken. Season with salt and pepper.

Serve the roast chicken with the *sawsawan* for drizzling over.

SERVES 4–6

1 × 1.5 kg (3 lb 5 oz) chicken, jointed, or bone-in chicken pieces
6 Asian shallots, halved, or 2 red onions, cut into thick wedges
8 garlic cloves, smashed
1 teaspoon sea salt
2 teaspoons muscovado or dark brown sugar
freshly cracked black pepper
80 ml (⅓ cup) Annatto oil (see page 256)

### COCONUT VINEGAR SAWSAWAN

1½ tablespoons *sukang tuba* (coconut vinegar)
1 tablespoon *kalamansi* or lime juice
½ teaspoon sea salt
¼ teaspoon freshly cracked black pepper
½ teaspoon white sugar

*After scouring the town for atsuete (annatto), I turn as I always do to our caretaker, Evalyn. 'You don't need to buy,' she tells me. Five minutes later, she arrives with a bilao (basket) filled with bristly heart-shaped pods from her neighbour's tree. They pop open easily to reveal red jewels, not yet ready for cooking, but perfect for the children to draw on the ground and colour their lips and cheeks in a blushing pink.*

# Steak with brown butter, citrus & bay leaves

## BISTEK TAGALOG

*Bistek* is quintessential home cooking (*lutong bahay*). Traditionally made with beef minute steaks and sweet white onion rings, it's quick to prepare and paired with mounds of warm, steamed rice, which soaks up the mouth-tingling salty soy and sour *kalamansi* sauce — perfect for big, hungry families. Derived from Spanish *bistec*, itself a loan word from English beef steak, Filipino *bistek* is symbolic of how we reimagined many foreign dishes with indigenous ingredients and oomph. Restaurants from Manila to Los Angeles are now elevating this humble dish with premium cuts and twists, like this version with browned butter inspired by Angela Dimayuga's recipe in the *New York Times*.

### METHOD

Heat 2 tablespoons of the oil in a large frying pan over medium heat. Cook the bay leaves and garlic for 30–60 seconds each side, until fragrant and golden. Transfer to a plate, reserving the oil in the pan. Cook the onion rings in batches, for 2 minutes each side or until golden and just tender, taking care to keep the rounds together. Add to the bay leaf mixture.

Heat the remaining 2 tablespoons of oil in the pan over high heat. Season the steaks generously with salt and pepper, then cook, in two batches, for 3–4 minutes each side for medium–rare or until cooked to your liking. Transfer to a serving platter and cover with foil.

Meanwhile, combine the citrus juices and soy sauce in a small bowl.

Return the pan to medium heat. Add the butter and cook for 3 minutes or until melted, nutty and fragrant. Add the soy sauce mixture and swirl the pan to combine. Cook for 1 minute or until warmed through. It will taste sour, salty and sharp. Remove from the heat.

Top the steaks with the bay leaves, garlic and onion rings, then pour over the sauce and serve with steamed rice or roast potatoes, if you like.

SERVES 4–6

80 ml (⅓ cup) olive oil
10 fresh bay leaves
1 garlic bulb, cloves smashed
3 white onions, sliced into 1 cm (½ in) thick rings
4 × 200 g (7 oz) scotch fillet steaks, at room temperature
sea salt and freshly cracked black pepper
80 ml (⅓ cup) freshly squeezed *kalamansi* or lemon juice
80 ml (⅓ cup) freshly squeezed orange juice
80 ml (⅓ cup) soy sauce
60 g (2 oz) unsalted butter
steamed rice or roast potatoes, to serve (optional)

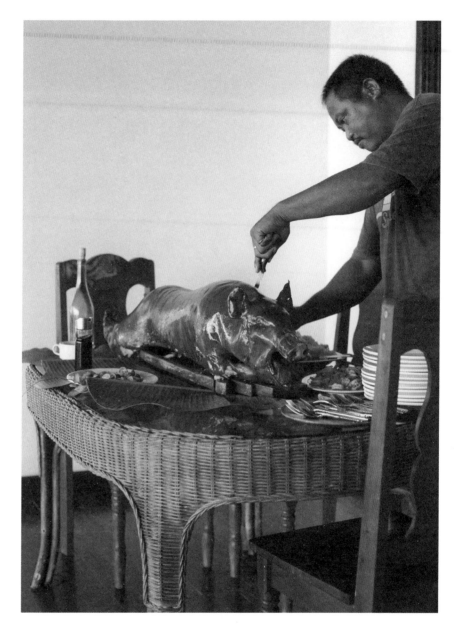

# Braised pork shoulder with pickled shallot sawsawan

When it comes to pork, we are reduced to our knees. Especially when it comes to *lechon kawali* and *crispy pata*, where a generous piece of pork belly or knuckle is first braised, then dried and finally deep-fried. It's a loving yet laboursome process with spectacular results, the cut both shatteringly crisp and meltingly tender. For years I named the two dishes as my favourites, but rarely cooked them, deterred by the multiple steps and spitting oil (yet not the enriching fat!). So one day, I tried slowly braising pork shoulder in oil over low heat instead of deep-frying. This is by no means like the traditional dishes, but it is absolutely arresting, layered with fragrant lemongrass, pineapple and whole garlic. If you've never braised in oil, you must try it at least once (think duck confit).

### METHOD

Place the pork in a stockpot or large saucepan and sprinkle over the salt and pepper. Add the garlic, lemongrass and pineapple and cover the pork with the oil. Set over low heat and bring to a gentle simmer, then cook for 4–5 hours or until the pork is meltingly tender. Alternatively, use a slow cooker. Remove from the heat and cool slightly in the oil.

Meanwhile, to make the pickled shallot *sawsawan*, place the vinegar, sugar, salt and pepper in a small bowl and stir to dissolve. Add the shallot and stir to combine. Set aside to pickle until needed.

Heat a chargrill pan over medium–high heat. Thinly slice one-quarter of the spring onions and stir through the steamed rice. Cook the remaining spring onions in the pan, turning occasionally, for 3–5 minutes, until tender and slightly charred.

Remove the pork and garlic wheels from the oil, and discard the oil, lemongrass and pineapple. Shred the pork into large chunks.

Transfer the pork, garlic wheels and charred spring onion to a serving plate and serve with the *sawsawan* and spring onion rice.

SERVES 6–8

3 kg (6 lb 10 oz) skin-on boneless pork shoulder, halved
2 tablespoons sea salt
1 teaspoon freshly cracked black pepper
2 large garlic bulbs, unpeeled, halved horizontally
4 lemongrass stalks, bruised
½ pineapple, peeled, quartered lengthways
2.5 litres (85 fl oz) sunflower oil
2 bunches spring onions (scallions), roots trimmed
steamed rice, to serve

### PICKLED SHALLOT SAWSAWAN

125 ml (½ cup) *sukang maasim* (cane vinegar) or rice wine vinegar
1½ teaspoons white sugar
1½ teaspoons sea salt
½ teaspoon freshly cracked black pepper
1 Asian shallot, finely chopped

Dried Fish

Soy Sauce &
Fish Sauce

Shrimp Paste

Salt Flakes

# *Alat*
# Salt

With seven thousand islands surrounded
by ocean, salt has always been a constant.

Our ancestors learned how to harvest
it from the water, then to preserve and
ferment fruits from the land and sea.

It developed our taste for not just salt,
but marine and pungent flavour.

Trade with the Chinese also introduced us
to soy sauce — black-brown, savoury and rich.

We call these ingredients the perfume of our
kitchen — one smell and we know if there
is too much or not enough, and feel at home.

# Pumpkin curry with young coconut & snake beans

## GINATAANG KALABASA

There are few greater pleasures than freshly pressed coconut cream or milk, which is inordinately sweeter, thicker and more memorable. With coconut palms at every turn, it's an affordable luxury born from a little effort: grating the mature meat with a *kudkuran* (coconut grater), then squeezing to release the thick liquor — the first, richer pressing known as *kakang gata* (coconut cream) and the second *gata* (coconut milk). *Ginataan* is our daily tribute to our beloved cream. Cooked with fragrant lemongrass, ginger and green chilli, it's a curry of sorts, but the sweet, rich coconut is the real star — even if you use tinned coconut cream like I have here. You can make *ginataan* with chicken, pork or seafood, but my favourite are the simple vegetable versions, like jackfruit or eggplant (aubergine), that cook in minutes for a nourishing lunch or dinner.

## METHOD

Heat 1 tablespoon of the oil in a large frying pan over medium–high heat. Add the pumpkin wedges, season well and cook for 8–10 minutes each side until golden and tender. Set aside.

Meanwhile, heat the remaining 1 tablespoon of oil in a separate large frying pan over medium heat. Add the ginger and lemongrass and cook for 30 seconds or until fragrant. Add the pumpkin chunks, stock and coconut milk, then season and bring to the boil over high heat. Cover, then reduce the heat to medium and cook for 13–15 minutes, until the pumpkin is very tender and almost breaking down.

Using a fork, mash the pumpkin pieces into the liquid until it turns orange (it's okay if it's not completely smooth). Add the coconut cream, sugar, chillies, coconut flesh and beans, then season and stir to combine. Bring to a simmer over medium heat and cook for 2 minutes or until the beans are tender but still with crunch.

Divide the pumpkin wedges and *ginataan* among bowls and serve with rice for a complete meal or as a vegetable side.

SERVES 4

2 tablespoons vegetable oil
1 kg (2 lb 3 oz) Japanese pumpkin (winter squash), half cut into 2 cm (¾ in) thick wedges, half cut into 2–3 cm (¾–1¼ in) chunks
sea salt and freshly cracked black pepper
5 cm (2 in) piece of ginger, peeled, thinly sliced
2 lemongrass stalks, bruised
375 ml (1½ cups) vegetable stock
250 ml (1 cup) coconut milk
250 ml (1 cup) coconut cream
1½ teaspoons white sugar
2 long green chillies
1 young coconut, flesh scraped into fat ribbons
300 g (10½ oz) snake (yard-long) beans or green beans, trimmed
steamed rice, to serve (optional)

*Each day I make my own coconut cream — much to the amusement of our caretaker. Squeezing with all my might, I yield a glass or so, but with a simple twist of the wrist and without breaking a sweat, she has three times the amount. We pour what's not reserved for cooking over ice cubes, torn mint and tarragon and sip our refreshing drink.*

# Watermelon & cucumber salad with fish sauce vinaigrette

## ENSALADANG PIPINO

Our salads typically feature only one or two ingredients. It could be a vegetable, fruit or fern; an unripe or mature specimen. We drench them in native vinegar, garlic and chilli, making them double as a side dish and dipping sauce for whatever we're eating. The result is a concert of simplicity and texture. With big bulbous cucumbers readily available at the market, *ensaladang pipino* (cucumber salad) is a favourite in most houses — quick and refreshing, and delicious with grilled meat and fish to cut through the richness. This is my colourful version with wedges of sweet watermelon, fragrant herbs and crispy fried shallots. Finished with a bright fish sauce vinaigrette, it's one of my favourite salads for entertaining. It's revitalising chilled, so prep all the ingredients, then keep in the fridge and pour over the dressing just before serving.

### METHOD

To make the fish sauce vinaigrette, combine the ingredients in a large bowl. Add the cucumber and refrigerate until needed or up to 1 hour to pickle.

Just before serving, strain the cucumber, reserving the vinaigrette. Place the cucumber, watermelon and herbs on a serving platter. Drizzle with the vinaigrette and scatter with crispy fried shallots to serve.

**SERVES 4–6 AS A SIDE**

2 Lebanese (short) cucumbers or 1 long cucumber, cut into 3 cm (1¼ in) chunks
¼ seedless watermelon, rind removed, cut into thin triangles
25 g (¾ cup) coriander (cilantro) leaves
15 g (¾ cup) mint leaves
crispy fried shallots, to serve

**FISH SAUCE VINAIGRETTE**

1½ tablespoons golden caster (superfine) sugar
1 garlic clove, finely chopped
1 bird's eye chilli, finely chopped
1½ tablespoons fish sauce
1½ tablespoons *kalamansi* or lime juice
1½ tablespoons *sukang maasim* (cane vinegar) or rice wine vinegar
1 tablespoon vegetable oil

*At first glance, they look like tiny grapes or immature olives, but their oblong shape and beautiful mottled skin require further enquiry. 'What are they?' I ask. 'Pipinito,' says the guide. The baby cucumbers pop in our mouths, releasing refreshing juice. Apparently they grow wild on the island, and my hunt begins.*

# Turmeric & cassia bark rice

## KIONING

Not a meal goes by that's not served with rice, whether freshly steamed (*kanin*) or glistening with garlic and oil (*sinangag*; see page 100). In the south, you'll often see it in yellow mounds, tinted and perfumed with turmeric — my eyes always gravitate to this beautiful sight. It's sometimes called Java rice, made famous by The Aristocrat Restaurant in Manila and owing to its similarity to Indonesian *nasi kuning*. Like much of the food throughout Mindanao and the Malay peninsula, the dishes are indeed related; *kioning* is the name given by the Maranao tribe, who shape their brilliant yellow rice into cone-shaped pyramids using banana leaves. It's variously enriched with lemongrass, cassia leaf or bay leaf, but this alluring version is scented with cassia bark and made creamy from evaporated milk. Make sure to use fresh turmeric — a far cry from ground when it comes to flavour. Once you try it, you won't want to make rice any other way again.

## METHOD

Heat the oil in a saucepan over medium heat. Add the onion, season with salt and pepper and cook, stirring, for 4 minutes or until soft. Add the garlic, ginger, turmeric and cassia bark or cinnamon and cook, stirring, for 1 minute or until fragrant and the oil is yellow. Add the rice and stir until well coated in the yellow oil.

Add the stock and evaporated milk and bring to the boil, then reduce the heat to low and cook, covered, for 12 minutes or until the liquid is absorbed. Remove the pan from the heat and stand, covered, for 5 minutes or until the rice is tender.

Pile the rice onto a serving platter or shape into individual mounds using a small bowl. Season with salt and pepper, drizzle over the extra evaporated milk and scatter with the micro coriander (if using).

**SERVES 6**

2 tablespoons vegetable oil
1 small red onion, thinly sliced
sea salt and freshly cracked
   black pepper
2 garlic cloves, finely chopped
3 cm (1¼ in) piece of ginger,
   peeled, finely grated
4 cm (1½ in) piece of turmeric,
   peeled, finely grated
1 cassia bark stick or ½ teaspoon
   ground cinnamon
500 g (2½ cups) jasmine rice
725 ml (24½ fl oz) vegetable or
   chicken stock
125 ml (½ cup) evaporated milk,
   plus extra to serve
micro coriander (cilantro) leaves,
   to serve (optional)

# Banana hotcakes with muscovado caramel & native lime

## INSPIRED BY MARUYA

We have numerous varieties of bananas, but our cooking bananas, known as *saba*, are used for daily *merienda* (snacks). Sometimes likened to plantain, they are sweeter and more moist, but still hold up really well during cooking. This makes them perfect for skewering and caramelising over flames (*banana-cue*), or rolling in spring roll wrappers with sugar and deep-frying (*turon*). These fluffy hotcakes are an ode to our sweet banana fritters known as *maruya*. Traditionally fried in batter and drenched in butter and sugar, these are infinitely easier to make at home; no cauldron of hot oil required, and made with whatever bananas you have on hand. Drizzled with golden muscovado sugar caramel and native lime, they're the ultimate indulgent breakfast.

### METHOD

To make the muscovado caramel, place the ingredients in a small saucepan over medium heat and stir until melted and combined. Remove from the heat and set aside.

Whisk the milk, egg, butter and lime zest in a large bowl. Sift in the flour, sugar, baking powder and salt and whisk again to combine.

Peel the bananas, then slice each banana lengthways into three slices, keeping them attached at one end. Melt a little butter in a small frying pan over medium heat. Add 60 ml (¼ cup) of the batter and swirl to coat the base, then top with one banana, fanning it out slightly. Pour over another 60ml (¼ cup) of batter and cook for 3–4 minutes, until golden and set on the base. Carefully turn the hotcake over and cook for a further 2–3 minutes, until golden and cooked through. Remove from the pan and repeat with extra butter and the remaining batter and bananas.

Divide the hotcakes among plates and spoon over the caramel. Scatter with the toasted *pinipig* and serve with the lime wedges.

---

SERVES 2–4

- 250 ml (1 cup) full-cream (whole) milk
- 2 eggs, lightly beaten
- 50 g (1¾ oz) unsalted butter, melted, cooled slightly, plus extra for cooking
- 2 *dayap* (native limes) or regular limes, zested, cut into wedges
- 150 g (1 cup) plain (all-purpose) flour
- 75 g (⅓ cup) caster (superfine) sugar
- 3 teaspoons baking powder
- ½ teaspoon sea salt
- 4 bananas (*saba* or cavendish)
- *pinipig* (pounded rice flakes), toasted, to scatter

MUSCOVADO CARAMEL

- 100 g (3½ oz) unsalted butter, chopped
- 75 g (⅓ cup) muscovado or dark brown sugar
- 60 ml (¼ cup) thickened cream

# Young coconut cream pie

## BUKO PIE

We have a special place in our hearts for *buko* pie. The warm flaky crumbs all over our hands and lips remind us of trips to Laguna province, where it's sold on every corner, or *pasalubong* (food gifts) from loved ones who've passed through there. Part American, part Filipino, its wildly delicious combination of golden, buttery crust with silky strands of young coconut came to life during the US occupation, when American baked goods were reimagined with native ingredients. I didn't think you could improve on the original — perfection with a scoop of vanilla ice cream (you can find the recipe in my first book *7000 Islands*) — but Manila cafe and bakery Wildflour's remake as a chilled coconut cream pie took my breath away. This is my version with luscious whipped pastry cream and milk powder crumbs.

### METHOD

To make the pie dough, place the flour, cornflour, sugar and salt in a food processor and process to combine. Add the butter and process for a few seconds until the mixture starts to come together. Combine the milk and vinegar in a jug. With the motor running, add the milk mixture and process until the dough comes together with large chunks of fat still visible. Wrap tightly in plastic wrap and refrigerate for at least 1 hour to rest.

Preheat the oven to 220°C (430°F). Lightly grease a 22 cm (8¾ in) pie dish.

Roll out the dough on a lightly floured work surface to a 27 cm (10¾ in) circle, about 5 mm (¼ in) thick, then use it to line the pie dish. Trim the dough so you are left with a 2.5 cm (1 in) overhang, then roll the overhang under itself and press it against the inner wall of the pie dish. Crimp decoratively. Place the pie shell in the fridge or freezer for at least 15 minutes so it is nice and cold.

→

**SERVES 10–12**

500 ml (2 cups) full-cream (whole) milk

500 ml (2 cups) thickened cream, plus 125 ml (½ cup) whipped to soft peaks

230 g (1 cup) caster (superfine) sugar

1 vanilla bean, split and seeds scraped

6 eggs yolks

50 g (1¾ oz) cornflour (cornstarch)

3 young coconuts, flesh scraped into thin ribbons (about 400 g/14 oz)

MILK POWDER STREUSEL

150 g (1 cup) plain (all-purpose) flour

80 g (⅓ cup) caster (superfine) sugar

30 g (1 oz) milk powder

¼ teaspoon sea salt

125 g (4½ oz) unsalted butter, softened, cubed

PIE DOUGH

250 g (1⅔ cups) plain (all-purpose) flour, plus extra for dusting

3 teaspoons cornflour (cornstarch)

1½ tablespoons caster (superfine) sugar

1 teaspoon sea salt

170 g (6 oz) cold unsalted butter, cubed, chilled

80 ml (⅓ cup) full-cream (whole) milk

1 tablespoon white vinegar

egg wash or milk, for brushing

Meanwhile, to make the milk powder streusel, combine the flour, sugar, milk powder and salt in a large bowl. Add the butter and toss to coat, then rub into the flour mixture until combined; it should be chunky and non-homogeneous. Refrigerate for at least 15 minutes or until chilled.

Prick the base of the pie shell with a fork, then line with foil. Fold the foil over the crimped edge, then fill the base to the top of the dish with pie weights (this prevents the crust slumping and shrinking).

Bake for 20 minutes. Carefully remove the pie weights and foil. Reduce the heat to 180°C (350°F). Brush the edge with egg wash or milk, then bake for a further 10–15 minutes, until the shell is cooked through and golden. Cool completely.

Line a baking tray with baking paper. Spread the streusel over the prepared tray in an even layer and bake for 8 minutes or until crumbly and golden in parts. Cool completely.

Meanwhile, combine the milk, cream, half the sugar and the vanilla seeds in a saucepan and bring to a simmer over medium heat. Whisk the egg yolks, cornflour and remaining sugar in a large bowl until thick and pale. Whisking constantly, add a little of the hot milk mixture until combined. Continue adding the hot milk mixture, little by little to temper, whisking until all combined. Return the mixture to the saucepan and bring to a simmer over medium heat, whisking constantly until thick and shiny. Remove from the heat and continue to whisk occasionally as it cools. Cover the surface with plastic wrap and refrigerate until chilled and set.

Fold the young coconut flesh into the pastry cream, then fold in the whipped cream. Spoon into the baked pie shell, then scatter over the streusel. Serve immediately or refrigerate for up to 3 days.

# Candied kalamansi cake

When asked what defines Filipino food, I always include *kalamansi*. Despite its diminutive size, our magical native citrus radiates with a floral fragrance and a sour, slightly sweet juice — somewhere between lemon, lime and mandarin. It grows everywhere and abundantly, which explains its presence in almost all our dishes and our love for tart, mouth-tingling flavours. By contrast, it's less commonly used in traditional sweet dishes. I'm not sure why, but this enigmatic cake with a buttery coconut base drenched in *kalamansi* syrup is my sweet homage to our sour jewels. Strictly speaking, the *kalamansi* isn't candied, which toughens its delicate skin and turns the glowing green brown. Instead, paper-thin slices are plunged into syrup, then poured over just before serving so it's beautifully thick and glossy. Buying fresh fruit is still difficult, but this cake is worth tracking down someone with a tree; if they're Filipino, they will always share their bounty with you.

## METHOD

Preheat the oven to 180°C (350°F). Grease a 20 cm (8 in) round cake tin and line the base with baking paper.

Whisk the flour, coconut, sugar, baking powder and salt in a large bowl. Whisk the melted butter, coconut milk, egg and *kalamansi* zest in a separate bowl. Add the wet ingredients to the dry ingredients and stir to combine.

Transfer the batter to the lined tin and bake for 45–50 minutes, until golden and a skewer comes out clean (if the top browns too quickly, cover the cake with foil). Transfer to a wire rack and cool for 10 minutes, then invert onto a serving plate.

Meanwhile, to make the *kalamansi* syrup, place the sugar and 125 ml (½ cup) of water in a saucepan and bring to the boil over high heat, stirring to dissolve the sugar. Reduce the heat to medium and cook for 12–15 minutes, until very thick and syrupy (if it starts to colour, you've gone too far). Remove from the heat and stir in the *kalamansi* juice. Cool slightly, then add the *kalamansi* slices and gently stir, just once, to coat.

Spoon the syrup and *kalamansi* slices over the warm cake and serve immediately.

SERVES 8

- 225 g (1½ cups) plain (all-purpose) flour
- 135 g (1½ cups) desiccated coconut
- 330 g (1½ cups) caster (superfine) sugar
- 2 teaspoons baking powder
- 1 teaspoon sea salt
- 250 g (9 oz) unsalted butter, melted, cooled slightly, plus extra for greasing
- 185 ml (¾ cup) coconut milk
- 3 eggs, lightly beaten
- 1 teaspoon *kalamansi* zest

CANDIED KALAMANSI SYRUP

- 230 g (1 cup) caster (superfine) sugar
- 2 tablespoons *kalamansi* juice
- 135 g (1 cup) very thinly sliced *kalamansi*, seeds removed

*A few times a year, my mum takes to her kalamansi trees, picking the fruit, then squeezing the juice for safe keeping in the freezer. The trees and fruit are small, yet there is always so much juice, which never fails to surprise me.*

# Purple yam jam

## UBE HALAYA

MAKES 750 G (1 LB 11 OZ)

500 g (1 lb 2 oz) *ube* (purple yam),
  peeled, cut into 3 cm (1¼ in)
  pieces (or use frozen *ube* pieces,
  thawed)
395 g (13½ oz) condensed milk
395 ml (13½ fl oz) evaporated
  milk
110 g (½ cup) caster (superfine)
  sugar
1 teaspoon vanilla extract
1 teaspoon *ube* flavouring
  (optional)

As *ube* shot to fame a few years ago, taking the global dessert world by storm for its natural bright purple hue, I couldn't help but feel a little vindicated. As a child, our delicious violet-coloured desserts were euphemistically called 'exotic' in Australia. Purple has always been our shade. A native yam, *ube* is at the heart of our most beloved desserts, from towering *ube makapuno cake* to sticky, Christmas-time *puto bumbong*. Its earthy, white chocolate flavour is subtle, often balancing the sweet elements it's paired with and building to obsession the more you eat it. *Ube halaya* is central to many of these desserts, swirled through *kakanin*, blended with ice and coconut milk for a refreshing shake or as the base for ice cream, or the crowning jewel on *halo halo* (see page 73). *Ube* jam, as it's often called, is not a jam in the true sense; more a sticky, sweet pudding or spread that you can equally eat by the spoonful. If you're using frozen *ube* which are typically paler, you can add a dash of colouring to boost its hue, but don't go neon as is the unfortunate norm of a lot of store-bought versions.

METHOD

Place the *ube* in a single layer in a steamer basket set over a saucepan of boiling water and cook for 25–30 minutes, until tender. Cool slightly.

While the *ube* is still warm, place in a blender with the remaining ingredients and blend until smooth.

Transfer to a saucepan and bring to a simmer over medium heat, stirring constantly. Reduce the heat to low and cook, stirring constantly to prevent scorching, for 30 minutes or until thickened to a creamy paste. Remove from the heat. Cover the surface with plastic wrap to prevent a skin forming, then cool to room temperature.

Use immediately or keep in an airtight container in the fridge for up to 1 week.

*I am an adult before I hold a fresh* ube *in my hands. It is long and bulbous, with dusty brown skin and a few curling tendrils — nothing special to see. I cut it open, a thin shield much like potato skin giving way to a glowing centre in rippled shades of amethyst and lavender. Unexpectedly, its flesh is sticky, unlike any root vegetable I know, but brittle and dry once steamed (the best way to prepare it). I am besotted.*

# *Gata*
## How to press coconut cream

3. Squeeze for kakang gata (coconut cream)

1. Open mature coconut

2. Grate meat with a kudkuran

4. Add water and squeeze again for gata (coconut milk)

# CHAPTER THREE

# Natural Beauty

FOOD WITH OUR HANDS

In the village, our neighbour knows which leaf to reach for this ailment or the herb teeming with *katas na mabisa* (life force). My cousin will tell you if a certain house has a friendly soul, then names the spirits — *aswang, kapre, engkanto* — best avoided. A friend can spot the sweetest young coconut palm from the limestone in the land, while another proudly recounts the tales of his heritage and tribe. Personally, I treasure this ancient, pagan way of life still widely practised, and the small pleasures we appreciate.

Similarly, our food is enduringly folk, natural and communal. There's the saucy *ulam* braised in clay *palayok* (pots) for aroma and flavour. The *sabaw* (soup) boiled in bamboo poles out of resourcefulness and now for savour. The smoky flames of *inihaw* (grilling) that kiss the meat and stoke our excitement. The banana leaves for transporting *baon* (packed meals) to work and the antioxidants that stop our food from spoiling. The bundles of *puso* (steamed rice) in sustainable nipa-palm pouches. The beautiful etchings on preserved fruit that please us, and the folded-leaf art on *suman* (sticky rice treats) that please the gods. And the single, shared glass of alcohol that unites and says we're one — your turn now, *tagay* (drink).

*Kamayan*, the traditional Filipino practice of eating not with fork and spoon but with the full feeling of the hands, is our ultimate paean to the environment. On tables lined with banana leaves, colourful mounds of food are piled in the centre to share, enhancing both flavour and experience.

These are the dishes that we enjoy with all our heart — an expression of beauty, each other and our surroundings.

# RECITES

# Puffed garlic & vinegar rice crackers

## INSPIRED BY AMPAW

SERVES 6–8

400 g (2 cups) jasmine rice, rinsed
   until the water runs clear
1 tablespoon vegetable oil, plus
   extra for deep-frying
2 tablespoons white vinegar
2 teaspoons sea salt

### SPICED COCONUT VINEGAR

125ml (½ cup) *sukang tuba* (coconut
   vinegar)
2 teaspoons white sugar
1½ teaspoons sea salt flakes, plus
   extra to scatter
freshly cracked black pepper
3 garlic cloves, finely chopped
2 small spring onions (scallions),
   white part thinly sliced, green
   part thinly sliced diagonally
¼ small red onion, finely chopped

Jonathan Bayad's plans to open a bar were all set when someone suggested serving Filipino food with a modern edge. I met Jonathan managing a restaurant I was profiling and we quickly connected over our heritage and Filipino cuisine's low representation in Australia. I gave him a copy of my first book, *7000 Islands*, and went on my way, none the wiser to what I'd implanted. A few years later, I received a message from Jonathan saying he'd done it. Rey's Place, which went on to have two Sydney venues at the time, also paved the way for other Filipino restaurants and opened the conversation about Filipino food in the country. These garlic-laden rice crackers are chef Nico Madrangca's savoury riff on *ampaw* — sweet crisp rice puffs — which he'd eat by the handful as a child. At Rey's Place, I love how he served them drowned in spiced *sinamak* (coconut vinegar) with sticky *longganisa* (see page 48). They're equally good with just the tart sauce, as the recipe here, or as a side to whatever you're serving. Think light-as-air salt and vinegar crisps!

### METHOD

Place the rice and 700 ml (23½ fl oz) of water in a saucepan and bring to the boil over high heat. Reduce the heat to low, cover with a lid and cook for 12 minutes or until the water is absorbed (the rice should be a little moist and sticky). Remove from the heat and stand, covered, for 5 minutes or until tender.

Meanwhile, preheat the oven to 240°C (465°F). Cut three sheets of baking paper the same size as three baking trays, then set the paper on a work surface.

→

*At Bankerohan, Davao's famous food market, there's temptation everywhere I look. Down this alley there's sticky* kakanin, *over here reams of noodles, and past piles of glistening peanuts I spy a childhood favourite. The vendor takes left-over cooked rice dried in the sun, plunges it in hot oil until puffed and crisp, then drenches the balls in caramelised sugar:* ampaw.

Combine the 1 tablespoon of oil, vinegar and salt in a small bowl, then stir into the rice.

Divide the rice mixture among the three sheets of baking paper, then top each with another sheet of baking paper. Roll out the rice using a rolling pin until about two grains thick with no holes. Transfer to the baking trays and remove the top sheets of baking paper.

Bake in the oven, rotating the trays halfway through cooking, for 30 minutes or until golden in parts and almost dry. Remove from the oven and set aside to cool.

Meanwhile, to make the spiced coconut vinegar, place all the ingredients except the green part of the spring onion in a small bowl and stir to combine. Set aside to steep until needed.

Fill a saucepan one-third full with oil and heat over medium–high heat to 180°C (350°F) on a kitchen thermometer. Break the rice into large shards. Working in batches, deep-fry the shards for 1–2 minutes until puffed, crisp and light golden. Drain on paper towel, scatter with salt flakes and set aside to cool.

Transfer the crackers to a serving board, scatter over the green spring onion and serve with the coconut vinegar to dunk in or drizzle over.

# Pickled green tomatoes

## ATSARANG KAMATIS

In the heat of the tropical sun, produce grows quickly, but passes its best just as fast. I am always taken aback by the speed of change and vibrant life force here. In Cagayan province in the country's south, ripe red tomatoes are preserved with garlic and pepper in bottles filled with salt to extend their life, known as *atsarang kamatis*. While *atsara* often refers to our classic pickle mix (see page 42), the word is a catch-all for our delicious preserves. I adore our green tomatoes, just-tart and so pretty, so I pickle them in native vinegar, which retains their firm bite and flavour. You can add them to salads, pour over eggplant (aubergine) omelette (see page 44) or serve as a side to grilled meats, the pickling liquid doubling as a mouth-watering *sawsawan* (dipping sauce). Or simply snack on them as I do straight from the jar.

### METHOD

Place the vinegar, sugar, turmeric and 250 ml (1 cup) of water in a saucepan and bring to the boil over high heat, stirring to dissolve the sugar. Cook for 2 minutes, then remove from the heat.

Sterilise a 1.5 litre (51 fl oz) jar and lid. Using tongs or clean hands, layer the tomato, ginger, chilli flakes (if using) and peppercorns in the jar, ensuring that it's not overfull (the brine needs to cover all sides of the tomato). Fill the jar with the hot brine until the mixture is completely covered, stir with a knife to remove any air pockets, then cover with extra brine if necessary; the mixture should reach 1 cm (½ in) from the top of the jar. Wipe the rim with paper towel, then seal with the lid.

Set aside in a cool dark place for 1 week before enjoying. Once opened, store in the fridge and consume within 2 months.

MAKES ABOUT 1.5 KG
(3 LB 5 OZ)

500 ml (2 cups) *suka* (native vinegar)
110 g (½ cup) caster (superfine) sugar
½ teaspoon ground turmeric
1 kg (2 lb 3 oz) small green tomatoes, sliced
3 cm (1¼ in) piece of ginger, peeled, thinly sliced
1 teaspoon chilli flakes (optional)
10 black peppercorns

*Every day at the local market is a surprise. Sometimes there are crimson heart–shaped tomatoes ready for sautéing into sweet ginisa (sofrito); other days they're mottled or a beautiful apple–green, their unripe flavour just right for sinigang (sour soup). I love the romanticism of it all, shaping how and what we eat each day.*

# Crab omelette with sour salad

## INSPIRED BY **RELLENONG ALIMASAG**

Even in the islands, blue swimmer crabs — known as *alimasag* — are a luxurious ingredient reserved for *fiesta*, when all the stops are pulled to make deliciously rich, crumbed stuffed crabs. I'm lazy, I'll concede, and this reimagination of *rellenong alimasag* as a rolled omelette is lighter, fresher and easier to make. It's also deliriously good; much like our *tortang talong* (see page 44), it's surprising how different and special an omelette can be. As the egg and soy sauce base hits the hot wok, it instantly puffs like a balloon, lending it a light texture that soaks up the bright sour *kalamansi* dressing. It's perfect for brunch with friends or an easy dinner tumbling with salad — just swap the crab for chopped cooked prawns (shrimp) or minced (ground) pork.

### METHOD

To make the sour salad, place the citrus juice, fish sauce and sugar in a bowl, season with pepper and whisk to combine. Add the tomato, capsicum, coriander or mint and spring onion and toss to combine.

Place the eggs, soy sauce and sugar in a bowl, season with pepper and whisk until just combined (you don't want the eggs to break up entirely).

Heat the oil in a wok or large frying pan over high heat until smoking. Add half the egg mixture and as soon as it starts to puff, gently lift the edges with a spatula to allow any uncooked egg to slide under. Cook for 40 seconds or until the base is golden and puffed, then carefully flip the omelette and cook for a further 20 seconds or until just cooked. Remove and drain on paper towel. Repeat with the remaining egg mixture.

Top with the crab meat or prawns, then roll up the omelettes. Top with the salad and drizzle over the dressing so most of it soaks into the omelettes. Serve immediately.

## SERVES 2–4

6 eggs
2 tablespoons soy sauce
½ teaspoon white sugar
freshly cracked black pepper
125 ml (½ cup) vegetable oil, for
    shallow-frying
150 g (5½ oz) cooked crab meat
    or prawns (shrimp), chopped

### SOUR SALAD

1 tablespoon *kalamansi* or lime juice
2 teaspoons fish sauce
½ teaspoon white sugar
freshly cracked black pepper
1 firm vine-ripened tomato, cut
    into thin strips
¼ red capsicum (bell pepper),
    very thinly sliced
handful of coriander (cilantro)
    or mint leaves
2 spring onions (scallions),
    shredded

*In the light of the moon, my children watch tiny crabs scuttle and scurry across the sand, before they're scooped into bags by night catchers. The next day, turned into deep-fried crispy crablets dipped in mouth-watering native vinegar, we savour them, then wait until the next catch comes around.*

# Barbecued pork skewers with black banana ketchup

John Rivera is one of Australia's best young talents. At just 26 years old, he became the executive chef of revered fine-dining restaurant Lume and used the platform to promote his Filipino heritage, combining technique and Australian produce in one. I fell for his food from the first bite, including this incredible version of our classic pork barbecue, cured with white, black and Tasmanian pepper and glazed in black banana *catsup* (ketchup). 'This dish has been with me the longest and I never get sick of it,' says John. 'I was often teased about Filipino banana ketchup at work, so I assured them that one of my signature offerings would be my own version and this is it. Made with black bananas, a technique of fermentation similar to black garlic, the process involves warming bananas for several weeks in a rice cooker on the "keep warm" function until rich and molasses-like. It's a lot more like an American barbecue sauce than our traditional bright red banana ketchup, but it's sweet, sour and spicy, just the way we like it.' Don't tell John, but I've also made it with overripe, almost black bananas. Either way, I use it on just about everything.

## METHOD

Place the coarsely crushed peppercorns, pepperberries, sugar and salt in a large shallow dish and stir well to combine. Add the pork belly and coat all over in the curing mixture. Cover and refrigerate overnight to allow the flavours to penetrate the meat.

Preheat the oven to 120°C (250°F). Line a baking tray with baking paper.

Place the pork on the prepared tray and roast for 1 hour or until the pork reaches an internal temperature of 70°C (160°F) on a kitchen thermometer. Remove from the oven, carefully place a large sheet of baking paper over the meat and weigh down with another baking tray. Set aside to cool.

→

## SERVES 6–8

1 tablespoon white peppercorns, toasted, coarsely crushed
1 tablespoon black peppercorns, toasted, coarsely crushed
20 g (¾ oz) Tasmanian pepperberries, coarsely crushed
55 g (¼ cup) brown sugar
70 g (¼ cup) sea salt
2.5 kg (5½ lb) skinless boneless pork belly
vegetable oil, for brushing

### BLACK BANANA KETCHUP

1 tablespoon vegetable oil
1 onion, finely chopped
3 garlic cloves, thinly sliced
¼ teaspoon ground white pepper
¼ teaspoon freshly cracked black pepper
¼ teaspoon ground cinnamon
¼ teaspoon ground cloves
¼ teaspoon freshly grated nutmeg
350 g (12½ oz) black fermented or very overripe bananas, roughly chopped
80 ml (⅓ cup) rum
250 ml (1 cup) *sukang tuba* (coconut vinegar)
100 g (3½ oz) grated palm sugar
100 g (3½ oz) treacle

To make the black banana ketchup, heat the oil in a saucepan over medium heat. Add the onion and garlic, and cook, stirring, for 4 minutes or until softened. Add the spices and cook, stirring, for 1 minute or until fragrant. Add the banana and rum and cook for 2 minutes or until the rum has almost evaporated, then add the vinegar, palm sugar and 250 ml (1 cup) of water. Bring the mixture to a simmer over medium–high heat, then cook for 25 minutes or until reduced by half. Add the treacle and cook for a further 5 minutes or until thickened. Remove the pan from the heat. While the mixture is still hot, transfer to a blender and blend until smooth (taking care to avoid the steam). Season with salt and pepper.

Preheat a barbecue to medium heat. Cut the pork belly into 2–3 mm (⅛ in) thick slices, then weave onto barbecue skewers. Brush with the oil, then generously brush with the black banana ketchup. Cook for 1–2 minutes each side, until warmed through and slightly charred. Serve with the remaining black banana ketchup.

# Beef skirt steak with charred tomato salsa

## INSPIRED BY TAPA

Sweet and salty beef *tapa*, a semi-dried beef jerky that's pan-fried until warm, is traditionally a breakfast dish, and one of our most loved at that. For me, the flavours used to marinate the beef also work wonderfully with steak and it's a number of steps easier — just toss in the marinade, then char on the barbecue. I like to use beef skirt, a textural cut that benefits from the vinegar and sugar, which help tenderise the meat, and looks impressive served whole or thinly sliced across the grain. We don't have a tradition of charring vegetables for *sawsawan* (dipping sauces), but I love the smoky, almost primeval depth it adds to the vinegar drizzle in this recipe. You can serve it with rice, as we love to do, or with crisp butter lettuce for wrapping and eating with your hands.

### METHOD

Combine the soy sauce, vinegar, sugar and garlic in a large shallow dish and season with pepper. Add the beef and turn well to coat. Cover and refrigerate for at least 1 hour or overnight to marinate.

To make the charred tomato *sawsawan*, heat a large frying pan over high heat. Add the tomatoes, shallot and bullhorn pepper and cook, turning occasionally, for 5 minutes or until softened and charred. Add the chillies and garlic and cook for 1–2 minutes, until slightly charred. Remove from the pan and set aside.

Place the vinegar, sugar and salt in a large bowl and stir to combine. Add the charred vegetables and, using a fork, gently press until slightly broken and chunky. Set aside until needed.

Preheat a barbecue grill to high. Remove the steaks from the marinade, drizzle with a little oil and cook for 3–4 minutes each side, until slightly charred and medium-rare or cooked to your liking. Set aside on a plate, cover with foil and rest for 10 minutes.

Thinly slice the steak across the grain (this ensures it's tender) and serve with the charred tomato *sawsawan*.

SERVES 4–6

125 ml (½ cup) soy sauce
80 ml (⅓ cup) *suka* (native vinegar) or rice wine vinegar
55 g (¼ cup) brown sugar
1 garlic bulb, cloves smashed
freshly cracked black pepper
800 g (1 lb 12 oz) beef skirt or flank steaks
vegetable oil, for drizzling
steamed rice or butter lettuce leaves for wrapping, to serve

CHARRED TOMATO SAWSAWAN

2 small vine-ripened tomatoes
2 Asian shallots, peeled, quartered
1 small red or green bullhorn pepper
2 bird's eye chillies
2 garlic cloves, peeled
80 ml (⅓ cup) *sukang iloko* (brown cane vinegar) or apple cider vinegar
3 teaspoons white sugar
2 teaspoons sea salt

# Maranao chicken curry

## PINDYALOKAN MANOK

SERVES 4–6

1.4 kg (3 lb 1 oz) whole chicken,
    jointed
sea salt and freshly cracked
    black pepper
60 ml (¼ cup) vegetable oil
125 ml (½ cup) chicken stock
    or water
200 ml (7 fl oz) coconut milk
3 dried bay leaves
2 teaspoons sugar
200 ml (7 fl oz) coconut cream
2 small green bullhorn peppers
    (optional)
2 long green chillies
steamed rice, to serve

### MARANAO CURRY PASTE

4 garlic cloves, smashed
1 tablespoon finely grated ginger
2 tablespoons finely grated
    turmeric
2 Asian shallots, finely chopped
½ bunch spring onions
    (scallions), thinly sliced
1 lemongrass stalk, white part only,
    pounded, finely chopped
4 bird's eye chillies, finely
    chopped
½ teaspoon sea salt

Over the years travelling through different regions in the Philippines, I'd always find chicken curry on restaurant menus, but could never track down the origins of the dish. Typically made with a curry powder–style base, did they simply spring to life from the blends now stocked at *sari-sari* (local stores), or was there a deeper history or connection I was still yet to find? Then, my friend Cathie Carpio took me into the heart of Quiapo district in Manila to try the oft-overlooked food of the Maranao tribe of Mindanao and I found what I had been looking for all these years. Made from a spice paste known as *palapa* (see page 179), generous with chilli, ginger, garlic and native spring onions (scallions) called *sakurab*, and braised with freshly pressed coconut milk and turmeric, it was golden, vibrant and magnificent. The Maranao people have a few iterations, including this wetter *pindyalokan manok* and a drier *piaparan manok* topped with grated coconut. Sadly, this dish is unlikely the inspiration of the chicken curries around the country, the Muslim-inflected, spice-laden cuisine of the south still yet to be discovered by many Filipinos. Yet the flavours here showcase our diverse history, and are one to behold.

### METHOD

To make the Maranao curry paste, place the ingredients in a large mortar and pound with the pestle to a fine paste. Alternatively, blitz using a small food processor.

Place the curry paste and chicken in a large bowl, season well with salt and pepper, and stir to coat. Cover and refrigerate for at least 1 hour or overnight to marinate.

→

Heat 1½ tablespoons of the oil in a large deep frying pan over medium–high heat. Remove the chicken from the bowl, reserving the curry paste. Working in two batches, cook the chicken pieces for 2 minutes each side or until golden. Transfer to a plate and wipe the pan clean.

Heat the remaining 1½ tablespoons of oil in the pan over medium heat. Add the curry paste, season with salt and pepper and cook, stirring, for 4 minutes or until fragrant and soft. Return all the chicken to the pan, along with the stock or water, coconut milk, bay leaves and sugar, then bring to a simmer. Reduce the heat to low and cook, covered, for 25 minutes or until the chicken is cooked through.

Transfer the chicken to a plate. Add the coconut cream to the pan, bring to a simmer over medium heat and cook, covered and stirring occasionally, for a further 15 minutes or until thick and oily. Return the chicken and resting juices to the pan, add the peppers (if using) and chillies and cook, covered, for a further 5 minutes or until the chicken is heated through and the peppers and chillies are just tender.

Transfer to a serving plate and serve with rice. Like all curries, it's even better the next day.

# Clam & corn soup with chilli leaves

## SUAM NA MAIS

SERVES 6

1 litre (34 fl oz) chicken stock
4 white corn or sweetcorn cobs, kernels stripped
2 tablespoons vegetable oil
1 red onion, finely chopped
4 garlic cloves, finely chopped
3 cm (1¼ in) piece of ginger, peeled, thinly sliced
1 vine-ripened tomato, chopped
4 long green chillies
750 g (1 lb 11 oz) small clams, soaked in cold water for 1 hour, drained
1 tablespoon fish sauce
handful of chilli leaves
freshly cracked black pepper

I spent a lot of time reading *Milkier Pigs & Violet Gold: Philippine Food Stories* researching this book. The author, Bryan Koh, spent six years bringing it together and I'm surprised it didn't take him longer; it's lyrical, expansive and exhaustive. He and I have since become pen pals and I asked him to share the recipe and story of one of my favourite dishes from the book.

"*Suam* is derived from two Hokkien words: *cu*, referring to the act of cooking, and *am*, a light broth made by simmering a small amount of rice in copious water. In the Philippines, it's usually delicately flavoured with vegetables and sometimes bolstered with meat or fruits from the sea. This particular suam is made with *mais* (corn); glutinous white corn tends to be preferred, the waxy kernels thickening the broth slightly, but you can use regular sweetcorn instead."

### METHOD

Place the stock and three-quarters of the corn in a food processor and process until almost smooth.

Heat the oil in a large saucepan over medium heat. Add the onion, garlic and ginger and cook, stirring, for 4 minutes or until soft. Add the tomato and cook, stirring, for 1 minute or until starting to break down. Add the chillies, stock mixture and remaining corn kernels and bring to the boil over high heat. Reduce the heat to medium and cook for 15 minutes or until the kernels are tender and the liquid is slightly thickened.

Add the clams and cook, covered and shaking the pan occasionally, for 3–5 minutes, until opened (discard any still shut). Remove the pan from the heat. Add the fish sauce and chilli leaves and stir until wilted. Transfer to serving bowls, season with pepper and serve.

# Chargrilled pork drowned in vinegar, cucumber & mint

## INSARABASAB

Known as *inihaw na liempo*, pork belly grilled over open flames is one of our greatest satisfactions. We wave fans over the simply salt and peppered pieces so the fire flares up and blesses the meat with smoke and char, then we submerge it in vibrant native vinegar or *kalamansi* juice, slicing it into pieces or taking bites with our hands in between. In the far north in Ilocos, this action of drowning the juicy pork in perky acid to cut through the richness is combined in one dish — *insarabasab* — and topped with fresh shallot, tomato and chilli. It's fabulous. When entertaining or simply for dinner, I use tender pork loin cutlets that tempt on the bone and pair them with a tumulus of pickled cucumber and refreshing mint. Other than big taste, eaten with a knife and fork it's also great for friends not accustomed to the delights of dunking and getting your fingers a little messy.

### METHOD

To make the cucumber and mint salad, place the vinegar, sugar and salt in a large bowl and stir until the sugar is dissolved. Add the cucumber, toss to combine, then set aside to pickle until needed.

Preheat a barbecue or chargrill pan to medium–high heat. Place the pork and oil in a large bowl, season generously with salt and pepper and stir well to coat. Cook the pork for 4–5 minutes each side, until golden and cooked through.

Meanwhile, place the citrus juice in a small bowl, season with salt and pepper and stir to combine. Transfer the pork to a plate and pour over the citrus mixture. Stand, covered, for 5 minutes to soak up the flavour.

Add the onion and finely chopped mint to the cucumber mixture and toss to combine. Divide the pork and cucumber and mint salad among plates and scatter over the whole mint leaves.

SERVES 4

- 4 pork loin cutlets (about 250 g/ 9 oz each)
- 2 tablespoons vegetable oil
- sea salt and freshly cracked black pepper
- 2 tablespoons *kalamansi* juice or half lemon and half lime juice

CUCUMBER AND MINT SALAD

- 60 ml (¼ cup) *sukang sasa* (nipa palm vinegar) or rice wine vinegar
- 2 teaspoons white sugar
- 1 teaspoon sea salt
- 4 Lebanese (short) cucumbers, thinly sliced
- ½ red onion, very thinly sliced
- 1 bunch mint, leaves picked, half finely chopped

# Pork belly adobo

## ADOBONG BABOY

After all these years, *adobo* still makes me swoon. The simple braise should be the same time and again, yet in the hands of each cook, it comes out wet and saucy or sticky and slightly sweet; laced with cane, nipa palm or coconut vinegar; infused with coconut milk, ginger, turmeric or annatto; and laden with chicken or pork, chicken and pork or a myriad of vegetables. It can be on the table within 15 minutes for a quick crisp *adobong kangkong* (water spinach) or bubble slowly for hours, rendering meat fork tender and the sauce rich and unctuous. With a generous slab of pork belly, this dish falls into the latter. The more common soy sauce is also replaced with fish sauce, lending it a beguiling salty marine flavour. For me, it's the ultimate entertaining dish — equal parts show-stopping and easy to make.

### METHOD

Heat 2 tablespoons of the oil in a large flameproof casserole dish over high heat. Season the pork belly flesh with salt and pepper, then cook for 3–4 minutes each side, until browned. Transfer the pork belly to a plate, reserving the oil in the dish.

Reduce the heat to medium. Add the onion, garlic and remaining 1 tablespoon of oil and cook, stirring, for 4 minutes or until softened. Return the pork to the dish, skin-side up, and add the fish sauce, vinegar, bay leaves and peppercorns. Bring to the boil, then reduce the heat to medium–low and cook, covered, for 45 minutes or until the flesh is tender.

Thickly slice the pork, then transfer to a serving plate and drizzle with the sauce. Season with pepper, scatter over the spring onion and serve with steamed rice.

### SERVES 4

60 ml (¼ cup) vegetable oil
1 kg (2 lb 3 oz) skin-on boneless pork belly
sea salt and freshly cracked black pepper
1 onion, cut into thin wedges
6 garlic cloves, smashed
80 ml (⅓ cup) fish sauce
310 ml (1¼ cups) *sukang maasim* (cane vinegar) or rice wine vinegar
3 dried bay leaves
2 teaspoons black peppercorns
2 spring onions (scallions), thinly sliced diagonally
steamed rice, to serve

Puto

Taro Leaves

Fermented Rice

Bitter Gourd

## *Pait at buro*
# Bitter and fermented

In the harsh dry terrain of the north,
our ancestors learned to make do.

In produce that took to the land, they came
to appreciate bitter, but also its undertone
of sweet.

Elsewhere, they observed ingredients first
deemed rotten shifting into something new.

By adding salt, they controlled the ferments,
making *buro* (fermented rice), *puto* (fermented
rice cakes) and *tapuy* (rice wine).

In our resilience and relationship with
the environment, we let nothing go to
waste — and find beauty.

# Coconut milk salmon with rainbow radishes

## SINUGNO

The marriage of coconut and fish is an ambrosial union.
In Bicol province, charmingly dubbed coconut country,
there's *ginataan na isda* (whole fish), *kinunot na isda* (flaked fish)
and *sinanglay* (tilapia wrapped in mustard leaves) to name a few,
variously infused with fragrant aromats. At my local fish market
on Siargao Island, there was always achingly fresh tuna, which
I'd buy in the morning, then braise in the evening, the sweet
coconut milk permeating the flavoursome flesh. Back home,
I like using salmon or ocean trout for its skin. I pan-fry it first
until it's golden and crisp, much like Quezon province's *sinugno*
(coconut milk grilled fish), then reduce the creamy sauce into
a rich, glossy glaze. It's sublime with a colourful radish salad
spiked with sesame oil or served simply with rice.

### METHOD

Combine the coconut cream, garlic, galangal or ginger, coriander root
and stem, sugar and fish sauce in a shallow dish. Add the fish, turn to
coat, then cover and refrigerate for 1 hour.

To make the radish and sesame salad, place the vinegar, citrus juice,
sesame oil and sugar in a large bowl, season with salt and pepper and
stir until the sugar is dissolved. Add the radish and chilli (if using)
and toss to combine.

Heat the oil in a large frying pan over medium–high heat. Add the fish
(reserving the marinade), skin-side down, and cook for 2–3 minutes,
until crisp. Turn over and cook for another 2–3 minutes, until just
cooked through. Remove from the pan.

Add the marinade to the pan and bring to a simmer. Reduce the heat to
medium and cook for 1–2 minutes, until warmed through and reduced
slightly. Remove the pan from the heat.

Divide the fish among plates and pour over the coconut glaze. Season
with pepper. Scatter the coriander leaves over the radish salad and serve
with the fish.

## SERVES 4

250 ml (1 cup) coconut cream
4 garlic cloves, finely chopped
4 cm (1½ in) piece of galangal
 or ginger, peeled, thinly sliced
¾ bunch coriander (cilantro),
 roots and stems finely chopped,
 leaves finely chopped
2 teaspoons white sugar
2 tablespoons fish sauce
4 skin-on salmon, ocean trout
 or tuna fillets (150–200 g/
 5½–7 oz each)
2 tablespoons vegetable oil

### RADISH AND SESAME SALAD

2 tablespoons *sukang maasim* (cane
 vinegar) or rice wine vinegar
2 tablespoons *kalamansi* or
 lemon juice
2 teaspoons sesame oil
2 tablespoons demerara sugar
sea salt and freshly cracked
 black pepper
300 g (10½ oz) rainbow or regular
 radishes, thinly shaved on a
 mandoline
2 bird's eye chillies, deseeded,
 finely chopped (optional)

# Crispy garlic & spring onion pancake with caramelised chilli jam

## INSPIRED BY UKOY

Laden with textures, from strings of green papaya and wispy mung bean sprouts to crisp school prawns (shrimp), our fritters, known as *ukoy*, turn ingredients on hand into lip-smacking deep-fried morsels. Depending on the cook's preference, they can be light and bite-sized, large and puffed or anywhere in between. We love to eat them as snacks at seaside restaurants, the cool breeze drifting in, while we sit with ice-cold beer, our hands going for one fritter, then another, dipping or drizzling with delicious *sawsawan* (dipping sauce) with each bite. Personally, I find their lacy shapes and cragged outlines so appealing. These oversized *ukoy* with thick chunks of garlic and long lengths of spring onion (scallion) look so beautiful, with fresh herbs and caramelised chilli jam over the top.

### METHOD

Place the flours in a large bowl, season generously with salt and pepper, and stir to combine. Place the soy sauce, stock and egg yolk in a separate bowl and whisk to combine. Add the wet ingredients to the dry ingredients and, using a fork, whisk 10–15 times, until almost combined (it will be a little lumpy). Cover and refrigerate for at least 1 hour to rest.

Meanwhile, to make the caramelised chilli jam, heat the oil in a small saucepan over medium heat. Add the red onion and chilli, season with salt and pepper and cook, stirring occasionally, for 8–10 minutes, until soft and almost caramelised. Add the sugar and cook, stirring, for 1–2 minutes, until caramelised. Stir in the vinegar, bring to a simmer, then remove the pan from the heat. Set aside to cool until needed.

→

## SERVES 4–6

150 g (1 cup) plain (all-purpose) flour
35 g (¼ cup) cornflour (cornstarch)
sea salt and freshly cracked black pepper
1 tablespoon soy sauce
250 ml (1 cup) vegetable stock, cooled
1 egg yolk, lightly beaten
8 garlic cloves, smashed
1 bunch spring onions (scallions), green and white parts cut into 5 cm (2 in) lengths
125 ml (½ cup) canola oil
large handful of coriander (cilantro) leaves
large handful of mint leaves

### CARAMELISED CHILLI JAM

1 tablespoon vegetable oil
½ red onion, finely chopped
2 long red chillies, thinly sliced
sea salt and freshly cracked black pepper
1½ tablespoons caster (superfine) sugar
60 ml (¼ cup) *sukang maasim* (cane vinegar) or rice wine vinegar

*It's the veggie pots that first have me fall for island life. Repurposed from old tins and lining house fences and ledges are rows overflowing with bright bok choy, spring onion (scallion) and other greens. If the market is closed, a neighbour kindly prises a bunch for me from the dirt to return the favour when needed.*

Remove the batter from the fridge (it will look like it has separated). Add the garlic and spring onion and stir to combine. Heat 60 ml (¼ cup) of the oil in a large 25 cm (10 in) frying pan over medium–high heat until the oil is shimmering and just smoking. Add half the batter and use a spatula to spread it over the base of the pan (don't worry if it doesn't reach the side and is an irregular shape, that's half the charm). Reduce the heat to medium and cook for 2–3 minutes, until golden and crisp on the bottom. Carefully flip the pancake and cook, gently pressing the pancake occasionally, for 2–3 minutes, until crispy and cooked through. Remove from the pan and drain on paper towel. Repeat with the remaining oil and batter.

Scatter the pancakes with the coriander and mint leaves, drizzle with a little caramelised chilli jam and serve immediately.

# Cabbage & green bean slaw with chilli-peanut dressing

## LUMPIANG HUBAD

Our spring rolls, known as *lumpia*, come in many guises. There's the classic, crunchy and oily (see page 226), the fresh *lumpiang sariwa*, made with a soft pancake or cabbage-leaf wrapper, and the delicate *lumpiang ubod*, a regional specialty filled with heart of palm, for which I shared a recipe in *7000 Islands*. There's also *lumpiang hubad*. Meaning naked, the vegetable-laden filling that's usually enclosed becomes the gratifying main act. Traditionally stir-fried with pork, I love the flavour and bite of simply crisp, fresh vegetables. Here, I've used colourful red cabbage, green beans and cucumber ribbons, but you can also add julienned carrot and charred marinated tofu to make it more substantial. As with all naked *lumpia*, the finishing touch comes with a punchy sweet and spicy peanut dressing.

### METHOD

Bring a saucepan of salted water to the boil. Add the beans and cook for 1 minute or until just tender, but still with crunch. Drain and refresh in cold water.

To make the chilli–peanut dressing, place the ingredients in a small bowl and whisk until well combined.

Drain the beans well. Place the cabbage, cucumber, onion, beans and half the dressing in a large serving bowl and toss gently to combine. Drizzle over the remaining dressing and serve immediately.

## SERVES 4 AS A MAIN OR 8 AS A SIDE

200 g (7 oz) green beans, trimmed, halved lengthways
½ red cabbage, thinly shaved on a mandoline
2 Lebanese (short) cucumbers, shaved into ribbons on a mandoline
1 red onion, thinly shaved on a mandoline

## CHILLI-PEANUT DRESSING

2 garlic cloves, crushed
1½ tablespoons chilli paste, such as sambal oelek
80 ml (⅓ cup) soy sauce
60 ml (¼ cup) *sukang maasim* (cane vinegar) or white vinegar
90 g (¼ cup) honey
1½ tablespoons chunky peanut butter

# Charred greens with coconut & palapa oil

Researching *7000 Islands*, very little was documented on the cuisine of the Philippines' far south and I was eager to learn and share more. It was through a friend in Manila that I got my first taste of the Maranao tribe's secret weapon: *palapa*, a condiment heavy with *sili labuyo* (chilli), ginger and *sakurab*, a spring onion (scallion) native only to Mindanao. You'll find grated coconut meat in some versions like mine here, adding scrumptious texture. In fact, *palapa* forms the base of most of their blazing dishes, including *pindyalokan manok* (chicken curry; see page 157), *rendang* (beef curry) and *phesasati-a-odang* (prawn and coconut cakes). Really, it can be used with almost anything with delicious effect, and made ahead and stored in the fridge so it's ready for action. Tossed through warm Asian greens, it's a scintillating vegetarian dish.

## METHOD

To make the palapa oil, place the oil, white part of the spring onion, ginger, chilli, sugar and salt in a saucepan over medium heat. Bring to a simmer, then reduce the heat to low and cook for 8 minutes or until the aromatics are tender and fragrant. Remove the pan from the heat, stir in the coconut and set aside until needed.

Preheat a grill (broiler) to medium–high. Line a baking tray with foil and add half the bok choy, gai lan, broccolini and spring onion greens in a single layer. Drizzle with 2 tablespoons of the *palapa* oil (without the coconut) and toss to coat. Grill, turning occasionally, for 3–5 minutes, until the greens are just tender, golden and lightly charred in parts. Transfer to a serving plate and repeat with the remaining greens. Drizzle with a little *palapa* oil (with the coconut) and serve.

The remaining *palapa* oil will keep in an airtight container in the fridge for up to 1 week.

## SERVES 4–6 AS A SIDE

1 bunch bok choy, halved or quartered lengthways
1 bunch gai lan (Chinese broccoli), halved or quartered lengthways
1 bunch broccolini, halved or quartered lengthways

## PALAPA OIL

250 ml (1 cup) vegetable oil
1 bunch spring onions (scallions), white part thinly sliced, green part reserved
2 tablespoons finely grated ginger
3 bird's eye chillies, deseeded if you prefer less heat, finely chopped
2 teaspoons caster (superfine) sugar
2 teaspoons sea salt
80 g (1 cup) freshly grated mature coconut

# Fragrant leaf rice

SERVES 6–8

2 tablespoons vegetable oil
1 large onion, finely chopped
8 garlic cloves, smashed
8 cm (3¼ in) piece of ginger,
  peeled, finely grated
2 teaspoons sea salt
2 teaspoons black peppercorns
400 g (2 cups) jasmine rice,
  washed until the water runs clear
5 fresh or dried bay leaves
40 g (1 cup) fresh moringa
  (drumstick) leaves (optional)

Each time I visit Bayatakan, I come home loaded with inspiration for uncommon ingredients and a full stomach. The organic community farm not far from our place in the northern foothills of Siargao runs in tandem with the Lokal Tabo market in town, growing and selling fresh produce and ensuring the livelihood for local farmers and food security for the island. It's also re-establishing native heirloom varieties and pioneering agri-tourism in the region with a pick, cook, re-plant approach and plant-based menus. It's so idyllic; on our last trip, we savoured a vegetarian feast *kamayan*-style (with our hands) in a wooden hut perched over the river, then cooled down in the water after lunch. This alluring rice was the star among many dishes. Steamed with the fresh leaves of chilli plants and drumstick trees known as *moringa*, or *malunggay* locally, the flavour is wonderfully peppery and unique. Depending on where you live, these fragrant varieties can be hard to get your hands on overseas, so you can make this with just bay leaves, another beloved leaf in the Philippines — and add moringa and chilli leaves if you can.

## METHOD

Heat the oil in a saucepan over medium–high heat. Add the onion, garlic, ginger, salt and peppercorns and cook, stirring, for 4 minutes or until soft.

Add the rice and stir for 1 minute or until well coated in the onion mixture. Add 700 ml (23½ fl oz) of water and the bay leaves and bring to the boil over high heat. Reduce the heat to low and cook, covered, for 12 minutes or until the liquid is absorbed. Remove the pan from the heat and stand for a further 5 minutes or until the rice is tender.

Add three-quarters of the moringa leaves (if using) and stir to combine. Taste, then season with salt and pepper. Transfer the rice to a serving platter. Scatter with the remaining moringa leaves and serve.

# Toasted flour blondies with cashews

## INSPIRED BY **POLVORON**

MAKES 12

260 g (1¾ cups) plain (all-purpose) flour
200 g (7 oz) unsalted butter, melted, cooled, plus extra for greasing
230 g (1 cup) caster (superfine) sugar
110 g (½ cup) brown sugar
2 eggs, lightly beaten
2 teaspoons vanilla extract
25 g (¼ cup) milk powder
1 teaspoon baking powder
½ teaspoon sea salt
100 g (⅔ cup) toasted cashews, roughly chopped

Bite-sized sweets hold a special place in our hearts. Shaped into little boats or pyramids or fingers or rounds, then wrapped in delicate pastel-coloured *papel de japon* (tissue paper) or colourful shimmering cellophane, they bring us beauty and joy as much as flavour. We gift them as *pasalubong* (food presents) from places we've visited and savour them one by one. Among the favourites are *pastillas de leche* (milk candies), *pili* nut tarts and peanut kisses, but no one can go past *polvoron*, our version of buttery shortbread. It's the flour that sets them apart, which is toasted before use until dark and nutty, as well as sweet milk powder. The flavour is really quite special and the inspiration for these moist golden blondies studded with cashews.

### METHOD

Preheat the oven to 180°C (350°F). Grease and line a 22 cm (8¾ in) square cake tin with baking paper.

Place the flour in a large deep frying pan over medium–high heat and cook, stirring occasionally, for 10 minutes or until fragrant and a dark golden brown (take care not to burn the flour). Remove the pan from the heat.

Meanwhile, place the butter and sugars in a large bowl and stir well to combine. Add the egg and vanilla extract and whisk until well combined.

Measure out 225 g (1½ cups) of the toasted flour, then sift it into a separate bowl with the milk powder, baking powder and salt. Add the dry ingredients to the wet ingredients and stir to combine.

Transfer the batter to the prepared tin and scatter over the cashews. Bake for 25–30 minutes, until the top is golden and a skewer inserted into the middle comes out clean (take care not to overbake so it's nice and moist).

Remove from the oven and cool, then cut into squares to serve.

# Banana leaf-baked sticky rice with coconut caramel & sesame

## BIBINGKANG MALAGKIT

You could dedicate a book alone to the history and varieties of our beloved native sweets known as *kakanin*. *Suman*, a catch-all for gloriously soft, stretchy, sticky rice wrapped in banana or palm leaves and a class of *kakanin*, is likewise deliciously voluminous. There's the black rice *suman de Baler*, the green rice *suman pinipig* of Bulacan, the lye water *suman sa lihiya* of Cavite, the chocolate *suman moron* of Leyte and the charred *suman tupig* of Pangasinan, to list just a few. And that's not even delving into the sweet dipping sauces and crunchy toppings they're served with. Although inherently simple — rice, sugar and coconut milk, wrapped, then boiled or steamed — like anything with a few ingredients, there's balance, technique and patience required. In each town, purveyors also shape *suman* into beautiful pyramids or parcels to please the gods. *Bibingkang malagkit* — baked sticky rice topped with luscious coconut caramel — is yet another subset of *kakanin* and this version, baked in banana leaves, is a nod to *suman* and the fragrance and beauty the banana leaves impart (but it is just as good without). For a variation, I also like warming pieces of sticky rice in a frying pan until slightly crisp on the edges, then dipping them in the delectable sauce.

→

MAKES 20

500 g (2½ cups) glutinous rice, rinsed until the water runs clear
2½ teaspoons sea salt
1½ tablespoons dark rum
banana leaves, to wrap (see page 257; optional)
2 teaspoons black and white sesame seeds

### COCO CARAMEL

625 ml (2½ cups) coconut cream
165 g (¾ cup) muscovado or brown sugar

*'You need long and gentle heat for* suman,*' says Tita Grace, as she finishes tying the last banana leaf knot around the pretty little bundles. 'This ensures the rice is fully cooked and renders the coconut milk, so it's more flavourful and aromatic.' A few hours later, we unfurl the native wrappers and the grains are glossy, supple, heavenly — and ready for the town fiesta.*

## METHOD

Cover the rice with water and soak for at least 2 hours or overnight. Drain.

Place the rice, salt and 750 ml (3 cups) of water in a saucepan and bring to the boil over high heat. Reduce the heat to low and cook, covered, for 10 minutes or until the liquid is absorbed. Remove from the heat and stand, covered, for a further 10 minutes or until the rice is almost tender.

Preheat the oven to 180°C (350°F).

Meanwhile, to make the coco caramel, place the coconut cream and sugar in a saucepan over medium heat. Bring to a simmer, then cook, stirring constantly, for 10–12 minutes, until reduced by half. Stir the rum and one-third of the coco caramel (about 185 ml/¾ cup) into the rice until well combined and glossy. Return the remaining coco caramel to medium heat and cook, stirring, for a further 5 minutes or until thick. Remove from the heat and set aside to cool.

Line a 1.5 litre (51 fl oz) glass or ceramic baking dish with banana leaves or baking paper, allowing the leaves to overhang by 15 cm (6 in). Spread the rice mixture evenly into the dish, then fold over the leaves or baking paper to cover. Bake for 1 hour or until light golden and sticky. Allow to cool completely.

Fold back the banana leaves or baking paper, spread the remaining coco caramel over the sticky rice, scatter with the sesame seeds and cut into pieces to serve. Alternatively, cut the sticky rice into pieces and serve with the coco caramel and sesame seeds for dipping.

# Tropical pavlova with burnt vanilla & lychees

SERVES 10–12

500 g (1 lb 2 oz) unsweetened coconut yoghurt
130 g (⅓ cup) drained *nata de coco* (coconut jelly)
80 g (½ cup) young coconut, flesh scraped into thin ribbons
400 g (14 oz) lychees, peeled and pitted
seasonal tropical fruit of your choice, sliced or chopped, to top
50 g (1¾ oz) coconut flakes, toasted

PAVLOVA

1 vanilla bean, split lengthways, seeds scraped, bean roughly chopped
6 egg whites, at room temperature
330 g (11½ oz) caster (superfine) sugar
3 teaspoons cornflour (cornstarch)
1 teaspoon white vinegar

This breathtaking pavlova is my tribute to the glorious tropical fruit of the Philippines. While we don't have a pavlova *per se* (that's the Australian in me), we have *paciencia*, *brazo de mercedes*, *canonigo* and a long tradition of light-as-air egg white creations, a vestige of Spanish colonial rule. With lychees, young coconut and *nata de coco* (coconut jelly) swirled through thick coconut yoghurt, the topping is inspired by *buko* salad. But the secret ingredient is really vanilla, which is 'burnt' by toasting a whole bean in a pan until intensely fragrant. It's unlike any vanilla you've tried before and a celebration of all of nature's bounty — pod, trimmings and all.

METHOD

Preheat the oven to 150°C (300°F). To make the pavlova, place the vanilla pod in a small frying pan over medium–high heat. Cook, stirring occasionally, for 3 minutes or until fragrant. Cool slightly, then grind in a spice grinder to a fine powder.

Meanwhile, line a baking tray with baking paper. Using a 20 cm (8 in) round cake tin, draw a circle on the paper, then flip the paper so the outline is on the underside.

Using an electric mixer, whisk the egg whites until just before stiff peaks. With the motor running, add the sugar, 1 tablespoon at a time, whisking until the sugar is dissolved and the meringue is thick and glossy (about 5 minutes). Add the cornflour and whisk for 1 minute, then add the vinegar, vanilla seeds and burnt vanilla powder and whisk until combined.

Spoon the meringue onto the baking paper circle and smooth the surface. Using a palette knife, drag the meringue from the bottom up into peaks. Reduce the oven temperature to 100°C (210°F) and bake the meringue for 1 hour or until set and hollow when tapped on the bottom. Set aside until completely cool.

Place the yoghurt, *nata de coco* and young coconut in a bowl and gently swirl to combine. Carefully pile the yoghurt mixture onto the cooled pavlova, then decorate with the lychees and seasonal fruit. Scatter with the toasted coconut flakes and serve immediately.

*As the sun beats down and the sea breeze sweeps through, the sweet nectar of mango, watermelon and young coconut water falls from our mouths as we sit cross-legged under the shade of a grand talisay tree. I can't imagine any time more perfect.*

# *Puso*
# How to weave rice pouches

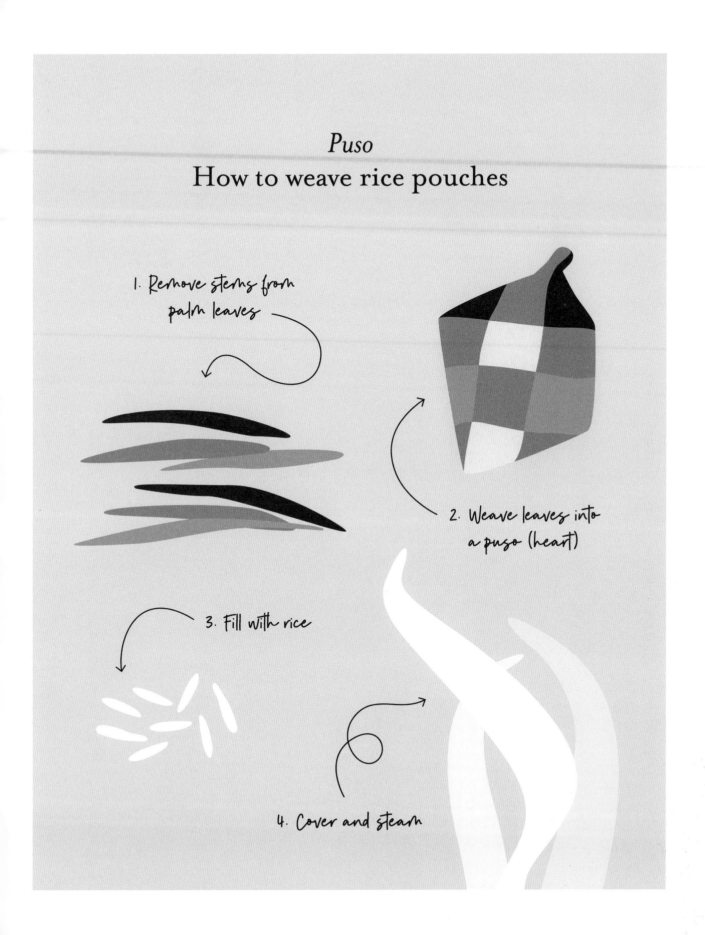

1. Remove stems from palm leaves

2. Weave leaves into a puso (heart)

3. Fill with rice

4. Cover and steam

# CHAPTER FOUR

# Memories

FOOD THAT CELEBRATES,
COMMEMORATES AND REMINDS

I love the lingering, palpable feeling of *fiesta*. In the weeks leading up to a *pista ng bayan* (town festival), the streets sparkle with brightly coloured flags that whirl in the wind. Before a wedding or christening, backyards bustle with tables, chairs and huts being built and the energy of extra hands. At the crack of dawn, neighbours arrive with a sweet birthday serenade; at midnight, it's the sounds of karaoke. And even as loved ones pass, days are spent both in mourning and joyful celebration.

Our life is simple, yet complete with the festive holy days and holidays of each month and passing year.

Known as *fiesta food*, our special dishes mark these occasions. The *pancit palabok*, laden with shrimp for happiness and noodles for long life. The *kakanin* (indigenous sweets) in decorative banana leaves that quell our native soul. The turmeric rice from pagan times with yellow to mark the heavens. The sticky *tikoy* (rice cake) to keep gods' mouths from revealing bad behaviour when Lunar New Year comes around. The Christmas ham, chorizo and *queso de bola* (Edam cheese) — once imported and reserved for the Spanish elite. The rich *ensaymada* (brioche) and *tsokolate* (hot chocolate) that warm chilly Christmas mornings. The *rellenong manok* (stuffed chicken) that's tedious and time-consuming, but carved elicits 'wow'. The smooth, delicate *leche flan* (creme caramel) best prepared with tender love and care. The *lechon*, our beloved whole roasted suckling pig started hours in advance, that's large enough to feed the whole family and a hungry crowd. And *pasalubong*, sweet somethings from distant towns to take you on the ride with me.

These are the memorable dishes that say today is one-of-a-kind or remind us of times gone by — the dishes that cause us to celebrate, commemorate and reminisce.

RECIPES

Fermented black rice sourdough
TINAPAY | 200

Drunken prawns with gin
NILASING NA HIPON | 205

Seafood noodles with garlic & annatto oil
INSPIRED BY PANCIT PALABOK | 206

Crispy fish tempura with sweet & sour sambal
ESCABECHE | 209

Pork meatballs with crispy chorizo & queso de bola
INSPIRED BY EMBUTIDO | 210

Slow-cooked lamb with tomatoes, capsicum
& green olive salsa | KALDERETA | 214

Muscovado-braised beef brisket
with garlic wheels 219

Lechon with shiitake & black rice stuffing
LECHON LIEMPO | 220

Bean sprout, black fungus & spring onion
stir-fry with hot & sour sauce
INSPIRED BY LUMPIA | 226

Caramelised sweet potato with coriander salsa
INSPIRED BY KAMOTE CUE | 230

Green beans with peanuts, toasted rice &
caramelised soy | INSPIRED BY KARE-KARE | 233

Smoked coconut rice with eggplant
BRINGHE | 234

Tofu pudding drowned in muscovado syrup
TAHO | 239

Pineapple butter sticky buns with cardamom sugar
| INSPIRED BY PASTEL | 240

Cassava & ube cake with young coconut sorbet
CASSAVA BIBINGKA AT BUKO SORBETES | 245

Mango trifle with rum syrup, cashew
brittle & lime | 248

# Fermented black rice sourdough

## TINAPAY

Chef John Rivera's approach to Filipino food has been endlessly inspiring for me. As a Filipino-Australian, he blends old and new flavours that feel both classic and completely new. John plans to open a new restaurant, but for the meantime, he shared his beguiling take on Filipino bread with fermented rice that I loved from the first bite. 'I have fond memories of eating *buro* every time I visited family in Nueva Ecija,' says John. 'The fermented rice was delicious – salty, sour, savoury. I knew I wanted to incorporate its flavour into our offering somehow, so I whipped it through butter to serve with bread. What a disaster! (You never really know until you try.) I still had about a kilogram of fermented rice, so I put it through a batch of wholemeal sourdough thinking, what's the worst that could happen? The next day, I baked the bread. The smell was intoxicating, but not like normal. It turns out the extra sugar content developed a beautiful crispy, caramelised crust, while the extra moisture meant the crumb was soft and pillowy – the best of both worlds. To top it off, the bread had a pleasantly unique flavour: mildly salty, addictively sour and very savoury. Sometimes the failures are even more important than the successes, and our bread is testament to that. I've made the fermented rice with a combination of grains – jasmine rice, which breaks down and boosts fermentation, brown rice for texture and flavour and black rice for colour and nuttiness, but you can use any single variety or mix of rice you like. Start a week ahead.'

→

### MAKES 1 LARGE LOAF OR 2 SMALL LOAVES

250 g (9 oz) sourdough starter (see below)

15 g (½ oz) sea salt

200 g (1⅓ cups) wholemeal (whole-wheat) flour

600 g (1 lb 5 oz) bread flour, plus extra for dusting

375 g (13 oz) fermented rice (see below)

vegetable oil, for greasing

### SOURDOUGH STARTER

1.75 kg (3 lb 14 oz) wholemeal (whole-wheat) flour

1.75 litres (60 fl oz) room temperature water

### FERMENTED RICE

200 g (1 cup) jasmine rice

200 g (1 cup) brown rice

200 g (1 cup) black rice

60 g (¼ cup) sea salt

## METHOD

To make the sourdough starter, place 350 g (12½ oz) of the flour and 350 ml (12 fl oz) of the water in a large bowl and stir to combine – it will be thick and pasty. Cover with plastic wrap and set aside in a warm place for 48 hours to begin the fermentation process.

On day three, place 350 g (12½ oz) of the starter in a large bowl and discard the remainder. Add 350 g (12½ oz) of the flour and another 350 ml (12 fl oz) of the water and stir to combine. Cover with plastic wrap and set aside for 24 hours to ferment. Repeat this process on days four, five and six. On day seven the starter is ready to use.

At the same time, make the fermented rice. Bring a large saucepan of water to the boil. Add the jasmine, brown and black rice, return to the boil and cook for 25 minutes or until the brown and black rice are tender (the jasmine rice will be overcooked, but this is okay). Drain.

Transfer the cooked rice to a clean airtight container. Add the salt and stir until well combined. Cover the surface with plastic wrap, then cover with the lid. Set aside in a warm place for 1 week to ferment; it will be slightly wet and sour.

To make the bread, place 250 g (9 oz) of the starter, salt and 450 ml (15 fl oz) of water in a large bowl and stir until well combined. Combine the wholemeal flour, bread flour and fermented rice in a separate large bowl. Add the starter mixture and stir to combine. Turn out the dough onto a lightly floured work surface and knead for 5–8 minutes, until sticky with a little structure. Alternatively, knead in a stand mixer fitted with a dough hook. Transfer the dough to a lightly oiled bowl, cover with plastic wrap and set aside in a warm place for 40 minutes to prove.

Using wet or oiled hands, with the dough in the bowl, grab the bottom of one corner of dough and stretch it up and out, then fold it over the top. Repeat with the remaining corners. The dough should now be tighter with a bit more structure. Repeat the proving and stretch-and-fold process another two times.

Grease and line a 25 cm × 17 cm × 12 × cm (10 in × 6¾ in × 4¾ in) loaf (bar) tin. Alternatively, grease two 22 cm × 12 cm × 6 cm (8¾ in × 4¾ in × 2½ in) loaf (bar) tins. Turn out the dough onto a floured surface and gently shape into a rough 30 cm x 25 cm (12 in x 10 in) rectangle (or two 25 cm/10 in x 22 cm/8¾ in rectangles if using smaller tins). With the shorter edge closest to you, fold over the top right corner, then the left corner to form a rough triangle shape. Roll the dough from the tip towards you until you reach the end, pressing the edge to seal. Place the dough log in the tin, seam-side down. Repeat with the remaining dough if making two small loaves. Set aside in a warm place for 1–1½ hours, until doubled in size.

Place a roasting tin on the bottom shelf of the oven and an oven rack in the middle, then preheat the oven to 270°C (520°F) or as high as it will go. Carefully fill the roasting tin 1 cm (½ in) deep with boiling water. Add the loaf tin/s, reduce the temperature to 240°C (465°F) and bake for 20 minutes. Reduce the temperature to 230°C (445°F) and bake for a further 20 minutes. Carefully remove the bread from the tin/s, place directly on the oven rack and bake for a final 5–7 minutes, until the crust is dark golden all over.

Remove from the oven and cool completely on a wire rack.

*Note: Save the left-over sourdough starter and fermented rice to make future batches of sourdough. The starter will keep in the fridge, following the process of replenishing with flour and water once a week. The fermented rice will keep in an airtight container in the fridge for up to 1 month.*

# Drunken prawns with gin

## NILASING NA HIPON

Leafing through *From Our Table to Yours*, written by my friend and food writer Angelo Comsti, I stumbled upon an old family recipe for *nilasing na hipon* – drunken prawns (shrimp) with gin. I love heirloom recipes. They tell such beautiful personal stories and recall flavours forgotten over time. And I just loved the sound of this dish: prawns marinated in booze, dusted in flour, then deep-fried until crunchy. It brought back memories of a dish my cousin would make and serve as *pulutan* (beer food), which had a toothsome oily sauce, but never had a name. This is my take on those delicious drunken dishes: abundant with garlic, onion and tomato (*ginisa* – our version of sofrito), and finished with a generous pour of gin. It's best shared in my opinion, savouring a few special plump prawns swirled in the glistening, unctuous liquor.

### METHOD

Heat the oil in a wok or a large deep frying pan over medium heat. Add the onion and all the garlic, season well with salt and pepper and cook, stirring, for 4 minutes or until soft. Add the tomato and cook, stirring and gently pressing the tomato, for 1 minute or until starting to break down.

Add the gin and bay leaves and bring to a simmer, then cook for 2 minutes or until the liquid is reduced by half. Increase the heat to high. Add half the prawns and cook, stirring, for 2 minutes or until starting to turn pink (don't overcook). Remove the cooked prawns, leaving the tomato mixture in the pan and repeat with the remaining uncooked prawns.

Transfer the prawns and tomato mixture to a serving plate, season with salt and pepper and serve.

**SERVES 4–6 AS A STARTER OR SHARED DISH**

80 ml (⅓ cup) vegetable oil
1 red onion, finely chopped
1 garlic bulb, half finely chopped, half smashed
sea salt and freshly cracked black pepper
1 vine-ripened tomato, finely chopped
250 ml (1 cup) gin
5 dried bay leaves
1 kg (2 lb 3 oz) raw king prawns (shrimp), peeled and deveined, tails intact

*'Sugpo!' Today, the* tindera's *call is extra sweet. On Christmas Eve, the icebox on his bike-cum-store is brimming with just-caught prawns. I buy a bowlful, plus another for our caretaker's family, and we spend the afternoon prising the shells from the fleshy bodies ready for the celebrations to come.*

# Seafood noodles with garlic & annatto oil

## INSPIRED BY PANCIT PALABOK

SERVES 3–4

No *fiesta* is complete without *pancit* in some shape or form, but the crown jewel of all our noodle dishes is undoubtedly *pancit palabok*. Laden with prawns, squid and crab fat, tinted royal red with annatto oil and laid out in a generous woven basket, it's luxurious and beautiful to behold — just the right marker for a christening, birthday or family get-together. Chinese in origin and in custom, *pancit* also represent longevity, so we leave the threads long for good measure. In *7000 Islands*, I shared a recipe for traditional *pancit palabok* with all the trappings. This version takes its inspiration from *palabok*'s everyday cousins — *pancit Malabon* and *pancit luglug* — and my time in the south, where pristine seafood and light, fresh flavours abound. In some ways, its simplicity and big flavour, silky in rich garlic oil, reminds me of an Italian *frutti di mare*. It comes together quickly, so have all the ingredients ready to go.

6 garlic cloves, thinly sliced
125 ml (½ cup) vegetable oil
1 teaspoon sea salt
400 g (14 oz) raw king prawns (shrimp), peeled and deveined, cut into 3 cm (1¼ in) pieces
6 spring onions (scallions), white part thinly sliced, green part shredded
80 ml (⅓ cup) fish sauce
3 teaspoons white sugar
250 g (9 oz) cooked *palabok* (round rice noodles) or rice vermicelli
½ bunch garlic chives, cut into 3 cm (1¼ in) lengths
freshly cracked black pepper
1 tablespoon Annatto oil (see page 256)
2 soft-boiled eggs, halved
½ bunch coriander (cilantro), leaves picked
4 *kalamansi* or 1 lemon, halved or quartered

## METHOD

Place the garlic, oil and salt in a small saucepan. Bring to a simmer over medium heat and cook, stirring occasionally, for 2 minutes or until fragrant (don't let the garlic colour). Remove the pan from the heat.

Strain 60 ml (¼ cup) of the garlic oil (reserve the garlic) into a wok or large deep frying pan over high heat until almost smoking. Add the prawn meat and stir-fry for 1 minute or until the prawn is just starting to turn opaque. Add the white part of the spring onion and stir-fry for 30 seconds. Add the fish sauce and sugar and bring to a simmer. Add the cooked noodles and garlic chives and cook, tossing, for 1–2 minutes, until well combined and the liquid is almost evaporated. Remove the wok or pan from the heat.

Transfer to a serving platter and season generously with pepper. Drizzle over the annatto oil and remaining garlic oil (with the garlic), then top with the egg, green part of the spring onion and coriander. Serve with the *kalamansi* or lemon for squeezing over.

*I love the inviting smile and special service of Tita Ellen as I walk past each morning, guarding the fish market in town. 'Tanigue (mackerel)?' I enquire. 'Mamaya,' she'll reply warmly if it's not already there. Later. And sure enough, as the sun sets and the fishermen come in, there's fresh gleaming fish waiting.*

# Crispy fish tempura with sweet & sour sambal

## ESCABECHE

Filipino-Australian chef Ross Magnaye and I met at the Melbourne Food and Wine Festival in 2019. Along with Jordy Navarra of Manila's Toyo Eatery and Nicole Ponseca of New York's Maharlika, we cooked up ten courses in a celebration of Filipino food. It was a dream. In every bite, you could taste each of our unique perspectives — a mix of heritage and new experiences. One of my favourite dishes was Ross's bright and punchy *escabeche*. Historically, the dish's origins are Spanish and Chinese; during colonial rule, sweet and sour fish served in Chinese restaurants was renamed in the Spanish tongue, a tribute or perhaps mistaken identity with their own citrus-fish *escabeche*. With light, crisp tempura and sublime sweet and sour sambal, this is my simplified take on his recipe.

### METHOD

Preheat the grill (broiler) to high. To make the sweet and sour sambal, line a baking tray with foil. Place the capsicum, tomatoes and shallots on the prepared tray and grill, turning every 5 minutes, for 15–20 minutes, until charred and blistered. Set aside to cool for 5 minutes, then remove the skins. Transfer the vegetables and chillies to a food processor and process until almost smooth.

Heat the oil in a saucepan over medium heat. Add the garlic and sautè for 1 minute or until fragrant. Add the puréed vegetables and the remaining ingredients and bring to the boil. Reduce the heat to medium and cook for 15 minutes or until thickened.

Fill a deep frying pan with 1 cm (½ in) of vegetable oil and set over high heat. Place the flour, cornflour, egg and soda water in a large bowl and stir until just combined (you want chunks of flour remaining). Season the fish generously, then, working in batches, dip the fish in the batter and cook in the oil for 2 minutes each side or until crisp and cooked through. Drain on paper towel.

Place the tempura fish on a serving platter and pour over the sweet and sour sambal. Scatter with the mixed capsicum and serve.

## SERVES 4

vegetable oil, for shallow-frying
100 g (⅔ cup) plain (all-purpose) flour
30 g (¼ cup) cornflour (cornstarch)
1 egg, beaten
185 ml (¾ cup) chilled soda water (club soda)
sea salt and freshly cracked black pepper
500 g (1 lb 2 oz) skinless dory fillets, cut into 60–80 g (2–2¾ oz) pieces
¼ each red, yellow and green capsicums (bell peppers), cut into 5 mm (¼ in) dice

## SWEET AND SOUR SAMBAL

1 large red capsicum (bell pepper)
2 large tomatoes
2 Asian shallots, unpeeled
2 bird's eye chillies, roughly chopped
1 tablespoon vegetable oil
3 garlic cloves, finely chopped
2 tablespoons *sukang tuba* (coconut vinegar)
2 tablespoons grated palm sugar
1 tablespoon oyster sauce
2 makrut lime leaves
sea salt and freshly cracked black pepper

# Pork meatballs with crispy chorizo & queso de bola

## INSPIRED BY EMBUTIDO

You can trace most of our special-occasion dishes, known as *pang-pista*, to Spanish colonial rule. Our celebratory traditions long predate those centuries, but the luxurious foreign ingredients and techniques of the time became forever etched in our *fiestas*. *Embutido* is one such dish. A descendant of the Spanish sausage of the same name, it evolved in the Philippines into an elaborate meatloaf, studded with chorizo, whole eggs and colourful capsicum (bell pepper) that are 'revealed' when sliced. While the look is somewhat dated now, it brings back such memories of my great aunt *lola* Lily, who painstakingly made it to mark our return each time. These generous pork meatballs with crispy chorizo, *queso de bola* (Edam cheese) and rich capsicum sauce is how I now savour the heart-warming flavours of *embutido* at home.

### METHOD

Place the tomatoes, onion, garlic, capsicum and carrot in a food processor and process until smooth.

To make the meatballs, place the ingredients in a bowl and season generously. Using clean hands, combine well, then roll into eight large balls or 12 smaller balls. Heat 2 tablespoons of the oil in a large deep frying pan over medium–high heat. Cook the meatballs, turning, for 3–4 minutes, until browned all over. Add the tomato mixture, 250 ml (1 cup) of water, the vinegar, sugar and bay leaves and season. Bring to a simmer, half cover with a lid and cook for 12–15 minutes, until the meatballs are just cooked through and the sauce is reduced slightly. Remove from the heat.

Meanwhile, heat the remaining 1 tablespoon of oil in a large frying pan over medium heat. Cook the chorizo, stirring, for 3 minutes or until golden and crisp. Remove from the heat.

Divide the meatballs and sauce among bowls, drizzle with the pickle juice and scatter over the chorizo, extra cheese and a few parsley leaves.

## SERVES 4

800 g (1 lb 12 oz) canned diced tomatoes
1 onion, roughly chopped
2 garlic cloves, peeled
1 red capsicum (bell pepper), roughly chopped
1 small carrot, roughly chopped
60 ml (¼ cup) olive oil
1 teaspoon *sukang iloko* (brown cane vinegar) or apple cider vinegar
2 teaspoons white sugar
5 dried bay leaves
sea salt and freshly cracked black pepper
2 cured chorizo sausages, finely chopped
80 ml (⅓ cup) pickle liquid (from jarred cornichons or dill pickles)
parsley leaves, to serve

### MEATBALLS

500 g (1 lb 2 oz) minced (ground) pork
80 g (2¾ oz) finely grated *queso de bola* (Edam cheese) or parmesan, plus extra to serve
60 g (¾ cup) coarse fresh breadcrumbs
½ onion, finely grated
1 garlic clove, finely grated
1 egg
sea salt and freshly cracked black pepper

# Slow-cooked lamb with tomatoes, capsicum & green olive salsa

## KALDERETA

In conversations about Filipino food, especially with the classics, there's always so much debate about what's traditional — usually with reference to one's mum or *lola's* version as the right and best way. The loyalty is endearing, but misplaced. Time and geography have crafted countless interpretations, not to mention personal taste. It's these differences that make food so fascinating and tantalising. With that preamble, this is my mum's *kaldereta*. Technically, it's not classic, made with lamb instead of beef and missing the liver sauce signature to many versions. In Australia, we lean towards lighter, fresher flavours and no doubt this influenced her cooking over the years. But it's *kaldereta* as I know it — and just how I like it. The lamb values from marinating overnight, taking on the vinegar flavour and tenderising the meat, but in a pinch you can throw it all in after an hour. My mum made this time and again entertaining family and friends. I've inherited the custom and it never fails to impress.

### METHOD

Combine the vinegar and half the garlic in a large non-reactive dish. Add the lamb, season generously with salt and pepper, then turn to coat. Cover and refrigerate overnight to marinate (or for at least 1 hour if pushed for time). Strain the lamb, reserving the marinade.

Heat 2 tablespoons of the oil in a flameproof casserole dish or large deep frying pan over high heat. Add the lamb and cook for 2–3 minutes each side until browned. Remove from the pan.

→

## SERVES 6

125 ml (½ cup) *sukang maasim* (cane vinegar) or white vinegar

8 garlic cloves, roughly chopped

1.5 kg (3 lb 5 oz) butterflied leg of lamb, meat scored

sea salt and freshly cracked black pepper

60 ml (¼ cup) vegetable oil

1 large onion, roughly chopped

400 g (14 oz) tin diced tomatoes

1 red capsicum (bell pepper), cut into 1–2 cm (½–¾ in) pieces

3 dried bay leaves

½ teaspoon chilli flakes (optional)

2 tablespoons tomato paste (concentrated purée)

200 g (7 oz) pitted Sicilian green olives, roughly chopped

steamed rice, to serve (optional)

Heat the remaining 1 tablespoon of oil in the same pan over medium heat. Add the onion and remaining garlic, season with salt and pepper and cook, stirring, for 4 minutes or until soft.

Return the lamb and any marinade to the pan, along with the tomatoes, capsicum, bay leaves, chilli flakes (if using) and 500 ml (2 cups) of water, then season with salt and pepper. Bring to the boil, then reduce the heat to low and cook, covered, for 1½ hours or until the lamb is tender.

Remove the lamb from the pan. Increase the heat to high and cook the sauce, stirring occasionally, for 20 minutes or until the liquid is reduced by two-thirds. Meanwhile, shred the lamb into large chunks.

Stir the tomato paste into the sauce and cook for 2 minutes or until warmed through, then remove the pan from the heat. Add the lamb and stir to combine.

Transfer to a serving platter, scatter over the olives and serve with steamed rice, if you like.

# Muscovado-braised beef brisket with garlic wheels

Muscovado sugar. Soy sauce. Garlic. When I think of these three simple ingredients, memories of some of my favourite dishes come flooding back — *humba*, *tapa*, pork barbecue. With different ratios and additions, they take on completely new shapes and forms, but that underlying holy trinity is there, entrancing our taste buds. While beef brisket is not a common sight, it's the perfect match to this mouth-watering combination of flavours — with pineapple juice or lemonade added for delicious depth — the cut slowly braising in the rich liquid mix until tender, sweet and savoury. It's also the perfect entertaining dish: easy to make in advance and feeds a crowd with steamed rice or piled onto warm flatbreads. Just a word of warning: your house will smell heavenly, so don't expect to be able to concentrate on anything else while it's simmering away. It's also *very* addictive.

## METHOD

Place the lemonade or pineapple juice, stock or water, soy sauce, sugar, salt and pepper in a flameproof casserole dish or large saucepan and stir to combine. Add the brisket and garlic; the brisket should be semi-submerged in the liquid.

Bring to the boil over high heat, cover with a lid, then reduce the heat to medium–low and cook for 2½–3 hours, until the brisket is fork tender and the liquid is reduced slightly and caramelised in flavour.

Thickly shred or slice the brisket, scatter with the chilli (if using) and serve with the flatbreads or rice.

SERVES 6

375 ml (1½ cups) lemonade or pineapple juice
125 ml (½ cup) beef stock or water
185 ml (¾ cup) soy sauce
110 g (½ cup) muscovado or brown sugar
3 teaspoons sea salt
3 teaspoons freshly cracked black pepper
2 kg (4 lb 6 oz) beef brisket, fat trimmed, cut into 10 cm (4 in) chunks
1 garlic bulb, halved horizontally
1 long red chilli, thinly sliced (optional)
Charred flatbreads with moringa leaves (see page 96), Turmeric and cassia bark rice (see page 120) or steamed rice, to serve

# Lechon with shiitake & black rice stuffing

## LECHON LIEMPO

SERVES 6–8

2 kg (4 lb 6 oz) skin-on boneless
  pork belly
sea salt and freshly cracked
  black pepper
1.25 litres (42 fl oz) chicken stock
  or water
200 g (1 cup) black rice
2 tablespoons vegetable oil, plus
  extra for drizzling
200 g (7 oz) shiitake mushrooms,
  thickly sliced
4 garlic cloves, finely chopped
Watermelon and cucumber salad
  (see page 117) or green salad
  leaves, to serve (optional)

There are few greater pleasures in life than our whole roasted suckling pig known as *lechon*. Requiring hours of tender love and care — preparing, then turning over coals to ensure the skin is perfectly crisp and the meat is succulent and tender — it's the centrepiece of our *fiestas* and savoured from head to toe. When a whole hog is too much, there's our *lechon liempo*. Much like Italian porchetta, pork belly is rolled, then roasted with equally crackling-meets-juicy effect, whether over traditional flames or in the oven. In the home of the flamboyant Dedet de la Fuente, aka Lechon Diva, I was treated to her world-famous *lechon* stuffed with truffle rice — hands-down the best I have ever tried. Inspired by the perfume it lent the meat, along with the side of rice used as a stuffing, this is my version with black rice and shiitake mushrooms, made *liempo*-style for home.

### METHOD

Score the pork belly skin in straight lines at 1.5–2 cm (½–¾ in) intervals. Scatter the skin with 1 tablespoon of salt, then refrigerate overnight (this helps dry the skin for an extra crisp finish; optional if you're pressed for time).

Bring the stock to the boil in a saucepan over high heat. Add the black rice and cook for 30 minutes to partially cook. Drain and set aside.

Heat the oil in a large frying pan over high heat. Add the mushroom and garlic and season generously with salt and pepper. Cook, stirring, for about 4 minutes, until golden. Remove from the heat, stir in the black rice and set aside to cool slightly.

Preheat the oven to 180°C (350°F).

→

*We order weeks ahead so the suckling pig is just the right size, as counselled by our neighbour. It arrives with two men on a motorbike on the morning of my daughter's birthday, then they wash the skin in coconut water and coax the fire to life. As the hours pass by, we take turns spinning its bamboo pole for perfect crackling skin, then set the centrepiece lechon on the table for everyone to appreciate and savour.*

Pat dry the pork belly skin using paper towel, then place skin-side down on a clean work surface. Butterfly the meat by slicing horizontally through the centre, stopping short of the end, then open to form one large piece.

Season the pork flesh with salt and pepper, then spread the black rice mixture over the skin-side down half of the pork. Fold the flesh over the top, then, with a long edge facing you, roll up the pork away from you into a log (the skin should cover the outside of the roll). Tie at six intervals with kitchen string to secure firmly.

Place a wire rack over a roasting tin and place the rolled pork belly on the rack, seam-side down. Rub with oil and season all over with salt. Roast for 1 hour 15 minutes. Increase the heat to 250°C (480°F) and roast for a further 30 minutes or until the skin is crackling and the meat is cooked through. Remove from the oven, cover loosely with foil and rest for 20 minutes before carving.

Mango

Rambutan

Durian

Heart of Palm

# *Tamis*
# Sweet

Our land has always flourished naturally with
sweet. In the heat of the equatorial sun and
thick tropical forests, our ancestors plucked
fruits and wild honey.

From native sugar cane and the sap of palms,
they turned sweet nectar into sugar, then used
it to sweeten *kakanin* (sticky rice cakes) and
preserve fruit in syrup.

With the colonial Spanish came sugar fields,
cacao and patisserie.

Sweet does not simply mean sugar. We savour
the teasing natural sweetness of heart of palm
or plump prawns — *manamis-namis*. While an
old Tagalog word describes the beloved sweet
lingering flavour of our meals — *himagas*.

# Bean sprout, black fungus & spring onion stir-fry with hot & sour sauce

## INSPIRED BY LUMPIA

SERVES 4 AS A SIDE

60 ml (¼ cup) vegetable oil

6 spring roll wrappers, quartered if large

1½ tablespoons sesame oil

4 garlic cloves, crushed

sea salt

100 g (3½ oz) fresh black fungus mushrooms, halved

100 g (3½ oz) water chestnuts, thinly sliced

½ bunch spring onions (scallions), cut into 3 cm (1¼ in) lengths

400 g (14 oz) bean sprouts

2 tablespoons soy sauce

### HOT AND SOUR SAUCE

55 g (¼ cup) caster (superfine) sugar

80 ml (⅓ cup) *sukang maasim* (cane vinegar) or rice wine vinegar

2 long red chillies, deseeded, thinly sliced

*Lumpia* (spring rolls) are synonymous with our *fiestas*. We make them in large numbers ahead of time, then deep-fry to serve, piling them high with a side of sweet and sour sauce for plunging into. As a child I loved the smaller, crunchier *lumpiang Shanghai* filled with pork and prawn (shrimp), and I'd grab handfuls with my cousins before running off to play. Now, I lean towards vegetable fillings generous with bouncy bean sprouts and cabbage. Truth be told, I'm also put off by the effort of deep-frying, especially for everyday eating. I prefer to savour them more like our naked *lumpia sariwa* — with a stir-fry of vegetables slippery with sesame oil and spring-roll wrappers crisped simply in a pan for crackling shards with each bite.

### METHOD

To make the hot and sour sauce, place the sugar and vinegar in a small saucepan and bring to the boil over medium–high heat, stirring to dissolve the sugar. Cook for 4 minutes or until slightly thickened. Remove from the heat, stir in the chilli and set aside.

Heat 1 tablespoon of the oil in a wok or large deep frying pan over medium–high heat. Cook the spring roll wrappers, in batches, for 15–30 seconds each side until golden and crisp, adding an extra tablespoon of oil as needed.

Heat the sesame oil and the remaining 1 tablespoon of vegetable oil in the wok over medium heat. Add the garlic and a pinch of salt and stir-fry for 30 seconds or until fragrant. Increase the heat to medium–high, add the mushroom and water chestnut and stir-fry for 1 minute. Add the spring onion and bean sprouts and stir-fry for 1 minute or until starting to soften. Add the soy sauce and cook, tossing, for 30 seconds. Remove the wok from the heat.

Transfer the stir-fry to a serving bowl and drizzle with the hot and sour sauce. Serve with the crisp wrappers on the side.

# Caramelised sweet potato with coriander salsa

## INSPIRED BY KAMOTE CUE

SERVES 4

1 tablespoon sweet paprika
2 tablespoons muscovado or light
    brown sugar
125 ml (½ cup) vegetable oil
sea salt and freshly cracked
    black pepper
1 kg (2 lb 3 oz) sweet potato,
    peeled if desired, cut into
    wedges
1 bunch coriander (cilantro),
    stems and leaves finely chopped
3 garlic cloves, crushed
2 teaspoons suka (native vinegar)
    or rice wine vinegar
2 teaspoons hot chilli sauce
1 teaspoon black sesame seeds
2 tablespoons pinipig (pounded
    rice flakes), toasted

Forever hungry, we have countless snacks on street corners to see us from one meal to the next. Enter sweet potato: ubiquitous, stomach-filling and comforting. We boil it in its skin to make soft *nilangang kamote* or fry in batter for crisp *ukoy*. When dusted in muscovado sugar to accentuate the sweetness, then deep-fried until caramelised, it becomes *kamote-cue* — a play on the word barbecue for the skewers it's served on — and hands-down the most popular rendition. While not traditionally served this way, caramelised *kamote* is such a natural star for a salad or vegetarian main. At home, I roast wedges in paprika and brown sugar, then drizzle over hot sauce and coriander salsa, with pops of black sesame and toasted immature glutinous rice flakes known as *pinipig* for crunch. It's sweet, savoury and moreish, just like our beloved *kamote-cue*. Filipino sweet potato is the purple-skinned, white-fleshed type, but you can recreate it with any sweet potato you have on hand, such as the orange variety I have used here.

## METHOD

Preheat the oven to 200°C (400°F). Line a baking tray with baking paper.

Place the paprika, sugar and 80 ml (⅓ cup) of the oil in a large bowl, season well with salt and pepper and stir to combine. Add the sweet potato and stir well to coat. Spread over the tray in an even layer and roast, tossing the sweet potato halfway through cooking, for 25–30 minutes, until golden and tender. Remove from the oven and set aside to cool slightly.

Place the coriander, garlic, vinegar and remaining oil in a small bowl, season with salt and pepper and stir to combine.

Transfer the sweet potato to a serving plate and drizzle with the chilli sauce. Spoon over the coriander salsa, sesame seeds and toasted rice flakes to serve.

# Green beans with peanuts, toasted rice & caramelised soy

## INSPIRED BY KARE-KARE

SERVES 4–6 AS A SIDE

80 ml (⅓ cup) Annatto oil (see page 256) or vegetable oil
100 g (¾ cup) redskin or regular unsalted peanuts
500 g (1 lb 2 oz) young green beans, trimmed
2 tablespoons muscovado or dark brown sugar
2 tablespoons soy sauce
freshly cracked black pepper
1½ tablespoons jasmine rice, toasted and ground to a powder
1 tablespoon freshly squeezed *kalamansi* or lemon juice

Many of the recipes in this book are vegetarian versions of classic dishes, and while some lean closer to the original, this adaptation of *kare-kare* is what you'd call inspired. A favourite among Filipinos, traditional *kare-kare* is a fixture at restaurants and *fiestas*, with hours needed to render the oxtail braise rich and unctuous. Instead, I've taken its signature ingredients — peanuts, toasted rice and *kalamansi* — and tossed them through green beans for a fast and fresh warm salad or vegetable side. Drizzled with caramelised soy in place of a spoonful of *bagoong* (shrimp paste), it's not at all like the original but altogether delicious and new.

### METHOD

Place the oil and peanuts in a small saucepan and bring to a simmer over medium heat. Reduce the heat to low and cook for 5 minutes or until golden and the flavour is infused. Remove from the heat and strain the peanuts, reserving the oil. Allow to cool slightly, then roughly chop the peanuts.

Meanwhile, bring a large saucepan of salted water to the boil. Add the beans and cook for 1–2 minutes, until just cooked and bright green. Refresh under cold water and drain well.

Place the sugar and soy sauce in a small saucepan and bring to a simmer over medium heat. Cook for 1–2 minutes, until reduced and slightly sticky.

Toss the beans, peanuts and oil in a serving bowl and season with pepper. Sprinkle over the toasted rice, then drizzle over the caramelised soy and citrus juice to serve.

*When school finishes each day, our home fills with countless children. They collect pipis from the beach, then show my kids how to boil and eat them. As I cook new dishes, they're always there watching and helping. I love these days with wide smiles and giggles and people always around me.*

# Smoked coconut rice with eggplant

## BRINGHE

You might not have guessed looking at it, but this is a descendant of Spanish paella. In genealogical terms, you could describe it as its grandchild, first transforming in the Philippines into *paella Valenciana*, then indigenising further to become *bringhe*, or native paella as it's sometimes called. It's incredible how far a dish can travel. Generously sized and slowly prepared, both dishes are wheeled out for *fiestas*. But while the former is more like the original with bomba rice (albeit tinted with local annatto in place of saffron), the latter is made with jasmine and *malagkit* — sticky rice — which mimics the soft, pillowy finish of the original. Hailing from the northern province of Pampanga, traditional *bringhe* is yellow with turmeric, laden with chicken and sausages, then cooked over low flames, forming a delectable crust on the bottom (*tutong*). In this vegetarian version studded with eggplants, I've replaced regular coconut cream with *sinunog sa gata* — smoked coconut cream. The result is beguiling, particularly paired with the banana leaf lid, which infuses additional aroma and flavour, but is just as good with regular coconut cream.

### METHOD

Heat 1½ tablespoons of the oil in a large deep enamel pan or large deep frying pan over medium–high heat. Season the eggplant with salt and pepper, then add half to the pan and cook for 2 minutes each side or until golden and tender. Remove from the pan, then repeat with another 1½ tablespoons of oil and the remaining eggplant.

→

### SERVES 6

100 ml (3½ fl oz) vegetable oil, plus extra if necessary
3 long thin eggplants (aubergines) or 1 small eggplant, cut into 1 cm (½ in) thick rounds
sea salt and freshly cracked black pepper
6 garlic cloves, smashed
1 large onion, thinly sliced
4 cm (1½ in) piece of ginger, peeled, finely grated
4 cm (1½ in) piece of turmeric, peeled, finely grated
300 g (1½ cups) jasmine rice, rinsed until the water runs clear
200 g (1 cup) glutinous rice, rinsed until the water runs clear
125 ml (½ cup) Smoked coconut cream (see page 257) or regular coconut cream
250 ml (1 cup) coconut milk
375 ml (1½ cups) vegetable or chicken stock
2 banana leaves, softened (optional; see page 257)
4 eggs (optional)
green salad, to serve (optional)

Heat 1 tablespoon of the remaining oil in the same pan over medium heat. Add the garlic and onion, season with salt and pepper and cook, stirring, for 4 minutes or until softened. Remove from the pan.

Heat the remaining oil in the pan over medium heat. Cook the ginger and turmeric, stirring constantly, for 1 minute or until fragrant and the oil is yellow. Add the jasmine and glutinous rice and stir until well coated in the yellow oil. Add the smoked coconut cream, coconut milk and stock and stir until well combined. Return the eggplant and the onion mixture to the pan and stir gently until well dispersed throughout the rice.

Bring the rice to a simmer over high heat, then cover with two banana leaves slightly larger than the pan and seal with the lid. Alternatively, just use the lid. Reduce the heat to medium—low and cook for 25 minutes or until most of the liquid has been absorbed.

If adding the eggs, make four egg-sized indents in the rice, then crack the eggs into the indents. Replace the lid and cook for a further 3 minutes or until the eggs are almost set and the rice base is golden and slightly crisp. Remove the pan from the heat and stand for 5 minutes. If you've used banana leaves, transfer them to a platter, then spoon over the rice in large scoops or serve straight from the pan. Serve with a green salad, if you like.

# Tofu pudding drowned in muscovado syrup

## TAHO

'*Taho!*' The street vendor makes us stop whatever we're doing and we beeline to his call. He ladles the delicate silken tofu into little cups, pours over the luscious brown sugar syrup called *arnibal*, then adds the finishing glimmering pearls. At 10 *pesos* a pop, it's a simple pleasure for an afternoon *merienda* (snack), as a drink-cum-dessert, or even for breakfast on the way to work. Chinese in origin, *taho*, derived from Hokkien *tau hau*, was once made with medicinal ginkgo seeds and chilli water, but with time in the Philippines it became replaced with local sweet flavours: sun-drenched muscovado sugar and tapioca and sago balls. Much like bubble tea in other parts of the world, *taho* comes in a kaleidoscope of colours today, like Baguio strawberry red and bright purple *ube*, but I love the classic here.

### METHOD

Place the tea leaves and boiling water in a small saucepan and steep for 5 minutes. Strain the liquid, discarding the leaves, then return the tea to the pan. Add the sugar and bring to the boil over high heat, stirring to dissolve the sugar. Reduce the heat to medium and cook for 8 minutes or until slightly syrupy. Remove from the heat.

Meanwhile, fill a saucepan three-quarters full with water and bring to the boil over high heat. Add the tapioca pearls and cook according to the packet instructions until tender. Drain, rinse under cold running water, then add to the sugar syrup.

Meanwhile, carefully place the tofu in a steamer set over a saucepan of boiling water and cook for 5 minutes or until warmed through. Remove from the heat.

Transfer the tofu to serving bowls, then pour over the syrup mixture and tapioca pearls. Serve warm or at room temperature.

SERVES 4–6

1 tablespoon oolong tea leaves
250 ml (1 cup) boiling water
220 g (1 cup) muscovado or dark brown sugar
100 g (3½ oz) black sugar tapioca pearls or regular tapioca pearls
250 g (9 oz) silken tofu, drained

# Pineapple butter sticky buns with cardamom sugar

## INSPIRED BY PASTEL

I discovered *pastel* years ago on the far-flung island of Camiguin, but my memory is so vivid it's as if it was yesterday. Limestone cliffs thick with tropical vines soared from the ocean's edge and white sandbars stretched as far as the eye could see — like a scene from *Jurassic Park*. And there in the heart of a small town was the softest, fluffiest brioche filled with luscious pineapple curd. *Pastel de Camiguin*, or simply *pastel* (the Spanish word for cake), began as an heirloom family recipe, but is now synonymous with this quaint and beautiful isle — a fitting match. Each time I think of that time, I'm instantly warmed, and these sweet morning sticky buns coiled with cardamom sugar and drenched in pineapple butter taste just like *pastel* and those breezy days — kissed by the tropical sun. Like all brioche, they are best eaten fresh within an hour from the oven.

### METHOD

To make the brioche, place the flour, sugar, yeast, salt, egg and milk in the bowl of a stand mixer fitted with the dough hook and knead on low speed until combined. Increase the speed to medium and knead for 5 minutes or until well combined. With the motor running, add the butter, one piece at a time, until combined, then knead for a further 8 minutes or until sticky and elastic.

Transfer the dough to a greased bowl and stand, covered, in a warm draught-free spot for 1–1½ hours, until doubled in size.

Meanwhile, grease and line a 22 cm (8¾ in) square baking tin.

To make the cardamom sugar, combine the sugar, cardamom and salt in a bowl.

→

MAKES 16

500 g (3⅓ cups) plain (all purpose) flour, plus extra for dusting

75 g (⅓ cup) caster (superfine) sugar

1½ teaspoons instant dried yeast

2 teaspoons sea salt

4 eggs, lightly beaten

100 ml (3½ fl oz) full-cream (whole) milk, lukewarm

225 g (8 oz) unsalted butter, cubed, softened, plus extra for greasing

### CARDAMOM SUGAR

110 g (½ cup) caster (superfine) sugar

½ teaspoon ground cardamom

½ teaspoon sea salt

### PINEAPPLE BUTTER

100 g (3½ oz) unsalted butter, cubed

165 g (¾ cup) caster (superfine) sugar

60 ml (¼ cup) pineapple juice

50 g (¼ cup) finely chopped pineapple (optional)

*When the table was piled high with brightly coloured boxes, we knew Tita was home. We opened them excitedly and gobbled up all the soft, crunchy and sticky sweets that came from afar. We call these food gifts 'pasalubong', moments from our travels that say I love you and share my experience with you.*

Lightly flour a work surface, then roll out the dough to a 65 cm × 30 cm (25½ in × 12 in) rectangle, with a long edge facing you. Lightly brush or pat the dough with water, then scatter over the cardamom sugar all the way to the edges. Tightly roll the dough into a log, sealing the edge on the bottom, then cut the log into sixteen 4 cm (1½ in) pieces. Place the dough pieces, cut-side up, in the prepared tin. Cover and stand in a warm draught-free spot for another 1–1½ hours, until doubled in size.

Preheat the oven to 180°C (350°F).

Bake the brioche for 35 minutes or until puffed and light golden, covering with baking paper for the last 20 minutes if they are browning too quickly.

Meanwhile, to make the pineapple butter, place the butter, sugar and pineapple juice in a saucepan over medium heat and stir until melted and combined. Bring to a simmer, then remove the pan from the heat and stir in the pineapple pieces (if using).

Cool the buns in the tin for 10 minutes, then slowly pour over two-thirds of the pineapple butter. Serve warm with the remaining pineapple butter.

# Cassava & ube cake with young coconut sorbet

## CASSAVA BIBINGKA AT BUKO SORBETES

I have told this story many times before, but it's worth sharing again here, along with the recipe for my mum's enduringly popular cassava cake. When I was a child, she would make her version of this beloved Filipino dessert and she quickly became known as the 'cassava queen' among friends and workmates in Australia, who'd never tried something so beguiling. It's now one of the most popular recipes in my first book, *7000 Islands*. Its charm comes from cassava, a root vegetable that once grated and baked becomes elastic and creamy, as well as the scorched condensed milk topping (*yema*) that sets it off. I've added thick *ube* jam for a striking twist, but it's equally good without. The same goes for the *buko sorbetes* (young coconut sorbet), but the combination of just warm cake and chilled coconut is sublime.

### METHOD

To make the young coconut sorbet, combine the sugar and coconut water in a saucepan. Bring to the boil over high heat, stirring until the sugar dissolves, then cook for 2 minutes. Add the coconut milk and cook, stirring, until the mixture comes to the boil. Transfer to a heatproof bowl, stir in the coconut cream and refrigerate until completely chilled. Transfer the mixture to an ice-cream machine and churn according to the manufacturer's instructions. Place in an airtight container and freeze until firm.

Preheat the oven to 180°C (350°F). Lightly grease and line the base of a 25 cm (10 in) springform cake tin with baking paper, then wrap the outside base in foil to catch any spills.

→

## SERVES 10–12

900 g (2 lb) frozen grated cassava, thawed
3 eggs
440 g (2 cups) caster (superfine) sugar
200 ml (7 fl oz) evaporated milk
300 ml (10 fl oz) coconut milk
60 g (2 oz) unsalted butter, melted, cooled, plus extra for greasing
250 g (1 cup) Purple yam jam (see page 130), or use store-bought *ube* jam

### YEMA

2 tablespoons plain (all-purpose) flour
395 g (13½ oz) can condensed milk
80 ml (⅓ cup) coconut milk

### YOUNG COCONUT SORBET

200 g (7 oz) caster (superfine) sugar
125 ml (½ cup) coconut water
300 ml (10 fl oz) coconut milk
400 ml (14 fl oz) coconut cream

Place the cassava, eggs, sugar, evaporated milk, coconut milk and butter in a large bowl and stir until well combined with no lumps remaining. Pour into the prepared tin, then dollop the purple yam jam over the top (it will sink slightly). Bake for 1 hour 20 minutes–1½ hours, until firm in the centre. Remove from the oven and leave to cool slightly.

Meanwhile, to make the *yema*, place the flour and half the condensed milk in a saucepan and stir to combine. Add the coconut milk and the remaining condensed milk and cook, stirring constantly, over low heat for 12–15 minutes, until thickened to a jam-like consistency. Remove from the heat.

Remove the cake from the tin, then pour the *yema* over the top. Using a kitchen blowtorch, scorch the topping. Serve warm or at room temperature with scoops of young coconut sorbet. If you're eating it the next day, warm briefly in the oven as it's best served elastic and springy.

# Mango trifle with rum syrup, cashew brittle & lime

In her essay, *Mangoes and Maytime*, treasured food writer Doreen Gamboa Fernandez lyrically conjures the special place *mangga* (mango) holds in our hearts. Its sweet perfume recalls childhoods by the river, where the sweet fruit would chill in the cold currents, or the farms where we'd eat it whole, the golden juice dripping down our chins and clothes. There are countless varieties in the Philippines, each prized for flavour, and without entering into a personal debate on which is the best, the *carabao*, or Manila mango, is listed in the Guinness World Records as the sweetest on earth. Our love for its ripe, sun-kissed flavour is immortalised in a number of classic and new desserts: mango shake, mango float, mango bravo to name a few. But the zenith is mango cake. With layers of light-as-air chiffon, delicate whipped cream and screaming sweet fruit, it's like a floating cloud struck with a ray of sunshine. I've tumbled it all into a trifle with cashew brittle, rum syrup and lime for pops of crunch and delight.

## METHOD

Preheat the oven to 180°C (350°F). Line the base of a 32 cm × 23 cm × 5 cm (12½ in × 9 in × 2 in) rectangular cake tin with baking paper (do not line or grease the sides).

To make the chiffon, sift the flour, baking powder, salt and all but 1½ tablespoons of the sugar into a bowl. Using a stand mixer with the whisk attached, beat the egg yolks, oil, 125 ml (½ cup) of water, lime zest and vanilla until combined. Add the flour mixture and beat on low speed until combined, then scrape down the side of the bowl. Increase the speed to medium–high and beat for 2 minutes or until thick and pale. In a clean bowl, whisk the egg whites until soft peaks form. Gradually add the remaining sugar and beat for 2 minutes or until stiff peaks form.

→

## SERVES 12

3 mangoes, cut into small dice
juice of 1½ limes
250 ml (1 cup) thickened cream, whipped to soft peaks

### CHIFFON

225 g (1½ cups) plain (all-purpose) flour
2 teaspoons baking powder
½ teaspoon fine salt
220 g (1 cup) caster (superfine) sugar
6 eggs, separated
125 ml (½ cup) vegetable oil
zest of 1 lime
1 teaspoon vanilla extract

### MANGO MOUSSE

2 mangoes, flesh scooped (about 400 g/14 oz)
170 g (¾ cup) caster (superfine) sugar
juice of ½ lime
1 titanium-strength gelatine leaf
185 ml (¾ cup) thickened cream, whipped to soft peaks

### RUM SYRUP

125 ml (½ cup) white or dark rum
170 g (¾ cup) caster (superfine) sugar
5 cm (2 in) piece of ginger, finely grated

### CASHEW BRITTLE

220 g (1 cup) caster (superfine) sugar
200 g (7 oz) roasted cashews

Using a balloon whisk or spatula, fold the meringue into the batter, in three batches, until well combined, taking care not to deflate the mixture. Transfer the batter to the prepared tin and run a spatula through the batter to prevent air pockets, then smooth the surface.

Bake for 30–35 minutes, until golden and domed above the pan (avoid opening the oven door too much or the fragile batter will deflate). Remove from the oven, cool for 1 minute, then invert the cake tin onto a wire rack (leaving the cake in the tin) and set aside for 1 hour or until completely cool.

To make the mango mousse, place the mango, sugar and lime juice in a food processor and process to a purée. Soak the gelatine leaf in cold water for 5 minutes or until softened. Place 125 ml (½ cup) of the mango purée in a small saucepan and bring just to a simmer over medium–high heat. Remove from the heat, add the gelatine leaf and stir until melted and combined. Transfer the gelatine mixture and remaining mango purée to a large bowl and stir to combine. Add the whipped cream and stir to combine. Cover and refrigerate for 1 hour or until slightly firm.

To make the rum syrup, place the rum, sugar, ginger and 185 ml (¾ cup) of water in a small saucepan. Bring to the boil, stirring to dissolve the sugar, then cook for 2 minutes or until reduced slightly. Remove the pan from the heat and set aside until needed.

To make the cashew brittle, line a baking tray with baking paper. Place the sugar and 3 tablespoons of water in a small saucepan over medium heat and stir until the sugar is dissolved. Increase the heat to high and cook for 5 minutes or until the mixture forms a golden caramel. Remove the pan from the heat and stir in the cashews until well coated. Immediately pour the mixture over the prepared tray and use a spatula to spread it out into a single layer. Cool completely.

To assemble the trifle, run a knife around the cake to release it from the tin, then cut into 4 cm (1½ in) triangles. Combine the mango and lime juice in a bowl. Finely chop two-thirds of the brittle, then roughly chop the remainder into bigger shards to decorate. Briefly dip one-third of the cake pieces in the rum syrup to soak all over, then place in a 3 litre (101 fl oz) trifle bowl or divide among individual serving glasses. Spoon over one-third of the mango and lime, dollop over one-third of the mango mousse and whipped cream, then scatter with one-third of the finely chopped brittle. Repeat the layering with the remaining ingredients, then top with the cashew brittle shards and serve.

# *Lechon*
# How to roast suckling pig

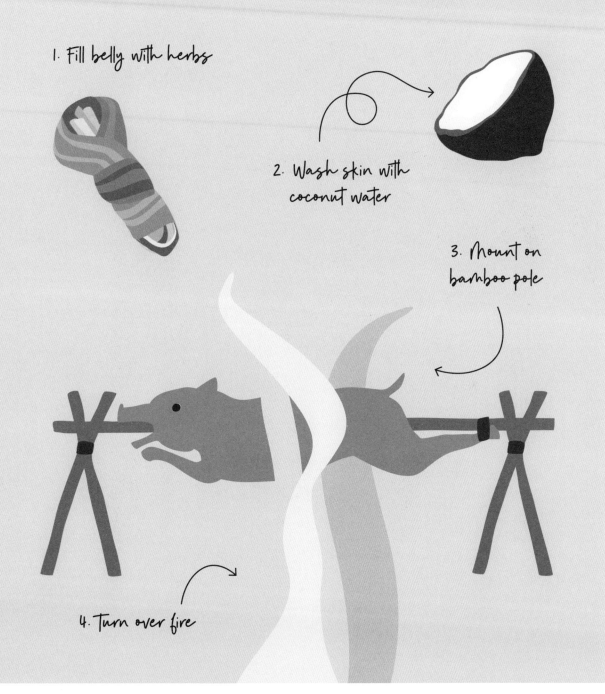

1. Fill belly with herbs

2. Wash skin with coconut water

3. Mount on bamboo pole

4. Turn over fire

# BASICS

## Annatto oil

**MAKES 125 ML (½ CUP)**

1 tablespoon annatto seeds
125 ml (½ cup) vegetable oil

Place the annatto seeds and oil in a small saucepan over low heat. Cook for 5 minutes or until the oil starts to turn red. Remove from the heat and stand for 20 minutes to infuse and release more colour. Strain, then use within a few hours for best flavour.

## Burnt coconut powder

**MAKES 2 CUPS**

1 mature coconut, flesh removed in large chunks

Preheat a gas barbecue to low or a chargrill pan over low heat. Add the coconut and cook, turning occasionally, for 40 minutes or until completely charred through. Cool completely. Transfer to a food processor and process, in batches, to a fine powder.

Burnt coconut powder will keep in an airtight container in the fridge for up to 1 month.

# Smoked coconut cream

MAKES 125ML (½ CUP)

500 g (1 lb 2 oz) grated mature coconut

Place the coconut in a large deep frying pan over medium heat. Cook, stirring occasionally, for 20 minutes or until dark golden and almost burned. Remove from the heat and allow to cool. Transfer the coconut to a bowl and pour over 250 ml (1 cup) of warm water. Stand for 10 minutes.

Line a sieve with muslin (cheesecloth) and set over a bowl. Pour in the coconut mixture, then lift up the muslin to form a ball and tightly wring to release as much liquid as possible.

Transfer to a jar and keep in the fridge for 1–3 days.

# Opening and grating mature coconut

Cut the coconut in half by holding it in one hand and striking firmly with the back (blunt side) of a heavy knife or cleaver, rotating the coconut and hitting around its equator until it splits. Whack the coconut halves with the back of a knife to loosen the flesh from the shell. Shred the coconut flesh using the large holes of a box grater or the shredding blade of a food processor.

# Preparing banana leaves

If using fresh banana leaves, look for thinner, more malleable leaves and remove the inner stem using a large sharp knife or scissors. If using frozen packaged leaves, defrost, then unfold. Pass each side of the banana leaves over the low flame of a gas burner until softened, glossy and bright green. Alternatively, pour boiling water over each side. Wipe the leaves clean and dry.

# Smashing garlic cloves

Using a large sharp knife, trim the ends of each garlic clove. Using the flat side of the knife, firmly whack or press down on the knife with your other hand to flatten each clove and loosen the skin. Remove the skin, then press again if necessary; the garlic should look minced and finely chopped in parts, with a few larger chunks remaining.

THANK YOU

It takes a village to raise a child and the same can be said of writing *Under Coconut Skies*. This is a thank you to the community that brought this book to life.

My beautiful family, Steve, Inés and Alejo, who packed up their bags for life on Siargao Island, then encouraged me as I wrote and tested recipes upon our return — and have always been my loving inspiration and support. My brother, Terry, and his partner, Krista, who came all the way from New York to the Philippines to pitch in. And my parents, John and Ruby, who were not able to join, but gifted me at a young age with a strong sense of identity and pride.

Evalyn and Jose, the caretakers of our home away from home, who exemplify Filipino hospitality, generosity and resilience, and who showed me countless age-old techniques and how to use ingredients from our surroundings. Also their nine children, whose smiles brought daily joy and care to our kids, which meant the world. Our friends Mark Pintucan and Iris Aroa, whose food preservation community work on the island is endlessly energising and important. Analyn Dulpina, proprietor of Bayatakan Farm, for her in-depth knowledge of native Filipino ingredients and sharing it with me, along with several recipes. Cathie Carpio, my fellow food history-loving friend, who took me into the heart of Mindanaon cuisine and proudly holds up the torch to spread the word further. Christopher Tripoli, Chris Uson of Filo Artisan Trade and Louie Cena of Auro Chocolate for guiding my way through Davao, where I learned so much from the country's rich southern food bowl.

My fellow Filipino food ambassadors for sharing your recipes with me – chef John Rivera, chef Ross Magnaye, Jonathan Bayad and chef Nico Madrangca of Rey's Place, chefs Alphonse Sotero and RJ Ramos of Lampara, chef John Kevin Navoa of Hapag, chef Dedet De La Fuenta of Lechon Diva and author Bryan Koh of *Milkier Pigs* – as well as Alvin Cailan, for his heartfelt foreword on our culture's cuisine, and long time friends and writers Felice Prudente Sta Maria, Angelo Comsti and Poch Jorolan for their ongoing inspiration and dedication to the preservation and elevation of Filipino food.

And to all the *carinderia* (local eatery) owners, *tindera* (vendors) and *kababayan* (countrymen) I met along the way, whose anecdotes and warmth provided another thread in the story.

Last but not least, the incredible team at Smith Street Books. This book would not have been possible without my publisher Paul McNally who believed first in *7000 Islands* and again in *Under Coconut Skies* and the importance of telling and sharing the story of Filipino food. My editor, Lucy Heaver, who expertly guided me along the way and shaped the book into these loving pages. Georgia Gold and Rochelle Eagle for the evocative food photography that captures the richness of our food, and stylist Deb Kaloper and cooks Caroline Griffiths and Meryl Batlle for bringing it so perfectly to life. Camille Robiou du Pont for the beautiful portraits set in and showcasing Siargao Island. Vanessa Masci for the poignant design and the magic and beauty it lends to all the words and recipes.

And to the Philippines, land of seven thousand islands and my beating heart.

Yasmin Newman was born in Sydney to a Filipino mother and Australian father, and aunts and uncles from around the world.

Each year, her family returned to the Philippines, where Yasmin and her brother spent long days bathing in the heat of the tropical sun, then cooling down with ice-cold *halo halo*; snaking through traffic on jeepneys to eat afternoon *merienda* or sneaking off with cousins at *fiesta* with hands piled full of crunchy *lumpia*.

In Australia, her mum prepared garlicky *silog* for breakfast, nourishing *nilaga* laden with rice for dinner and sticky–sweet *cassava bibingka* when friends came by.

In each delicious mouthful, the Philippines and its story was lovingly imbued and conveyed.

These experiences set Yasmin's life in one direction, with food — and the cultural language, family memories and sweeping history held in each dish — its driving force.

Over the last 20 years, she has lived worldwide, from Paris and Los Angeles to Mexico and the Philippines, exploring different cuisines and cultures.

As a food and travel writer and photographer, Yasmin has worked for leading Australian media including *SBS*, *delicious.* and *MasterChef* and has been featured globally in *National Geographic*, Oprah.com and *Vogue*.

Her first award-winning cookbook, *7000 Islands: A Food Portrait of the Philippines*, was first published in 2013 and in 2019 in a new edition. Her second book, *The Desserts of New York: And How to Eat Them All* was published in 2016.

On a trip to Peru, she met her Australian husband. They live on Australia's Central Coast with their two young kids, but return each year to the Philippines and Julita, their villa named after Yasmin's *lola* (grandmother) on Siargao Island in the idyllic south.

*Under Coconut Skies* is Yasmin's third cookbook.

# INDEX

**Smith Street Books**

Published in 2021 by Smith Street Books
Naarm | Melbourne | Australia
smithstreetbooks.com

ISBN: 978-1-92581-168-1

Text © Yasmin Newman
Design © Smith Street Books
Food photography © Georgia Gold and Rochelle Eagle
Location and portrait photography © Yasmin Newman

Publisher: Paul McNally
Senior editor: Lucy Heaver, Tusk studio
Designer: Vanessa Masci
Layout: Megan Ellis
Location photography: Yasmin Newman
Portrait photography: Camille Robiou du Pont
Food photography: Georgia Gold and Rochelle Eagle
Food preparation: Caroline Griffiths and Meryl Batlle
Proofreader: Pamela Dunne
Indexer: Helena Holmgren
Printed & bound in China by C&C Offset Printing Co., Ltd

Book 179
10 9 8 7 6 5 4 3 2 1